What *El Paso* readers said

about "1998: Year of the Family," the daily column from which these stories were collected:

I love "Year of the Family." I have never seen prayers and stories like these in a newspaper until I moved here last year. It's so uplifting to see this in print. I don't even read the news. The first thing I go to is the "Living" section.
Alana Lendvay, El Paso, TX

At a time when the "Clinton-Lewinsky Chronicles" saturate the news, it is refreshing to discover a column in the Times devoted to old-fashioned values, and a down-to-earth recipe for finding peace in a very troubled world. I am referring to "1998: Year of the Family" in the "Living" section. What a delight to read something wholesome, positive and encouraging for a change. The experts say that good news doesn't sell, but I can assure you that many of your readers are cheering you on from the sidelines.
Vernelle Harder, El Paso, TX

"Year of the Family" has been a tremendous blessing to my family and me! I've made a point of trying to read the column in the newspaper every day, even if I don't have time to read the rest of the newspaper. My husband also reads the column every day. I find myself cutting the column out at least once a week and tucking it away in my keepsakes folder.
Gretchen Runkle, Canutillo, TX

My mom and dad send me the "family" articles all the time and I have thoroughly enjoyed them. I would really appreciate hearing about the collection as I know many people who would enjoy reading these articles, too. Thanks for such inspirational writings—I was really moved by many of them.
Melanie Barco Cage, Houston, TX

These stories lifted my spirit and strengthened my hope for what to me often seems a very weary world.
Sally Kmetz, Albuquerque, NM

Your column made a difference in my everyday life. It seemed like the articles were talking about me, or like it was something I went through....
Sandra Betancourt, El Paso, TX

Thank you for publishing the "1998: Year of the Family" column. Our family looked forward each day to reading something so positive and uplifting, and we feel that each column brightened the day ahead. Please continue to provide us with inspiring, family-centered material as it becomes available.
Pat Fischer, El Paso, TX

We are sorry to see this column end. It is often the first item which we read. Reading the stories has been a source of inspiration and a welcome break from the usual newspaper fare. We would prefer that the column be continued as a regular feature.
Ben Narbuth, El Paso, TX

I really love your column and am sad to see it end. I have been reading your column in the *El Paso Times*, which we subscribe to on Sundays, and your column has made a big difference in my life and others I have passed it on to. Many thanks and God Bless!
Ann Terrazas, Schaumburg, IL

I tried to read the articles in the "1998: Year of the Family" series whenever I had opportunity and piled them up and saved them to read later—usually at early morning dawn. Although I was disheartened to read they are concluding, I was thrilled to read they would be compiled in a collection.
Yolanda Brown, El Paso, TX

My Roots Go Back to Loving
and other stories from "Year of the Family"

Want to know more about Year of the Family?

Year of the Family is an interdenominational Christian organization that grew out of the "1998: Year of the Family" project. It is dedicated to uniting communities for and through the task of teaching values that strengthen families. The community newspaper column modeled by this book is just one of many suggested projects that communities can use to accomplish this goal.

Address: Year of the Family
% El Paso for Jesus
P.O. Box 221212
El Paso, TX 79913
Phone: (915) 585-3787
Fax: (915) 566-7776

"Every year is the Year of the Family."

My Roots Go Back to Loving
and other stories from "Year of the Family"

Becky Cerling Powers, Editor

Canaan Home Communications
H.C. 12 Box 87
Anthony, TX 79821

© 2000 by El Paso for Jesus
All rights reserved. Printed in the United States of America.
Library of Congress Catalog Card Number: 99-74586
ISBN: 0-9672134-1-X
No part of this publication may be reproduced in any form without written permission from El Paso for Jesus, Attention: Year of the Family, P.O. Box 221212, El Paso, TX 79913
Cover photograph: Becky Cerling Powers
Cover design: Gloria Williams-Méndez

All scripture, unless otherwise indicated, is taken from the HOLY BIBLE, NEW INTERNATIONAL VERSION, copyright 1973, 1978, 1984 by International Bible Society. "NIV" and "New International Version" are registered in the United States Patent and Trademark Office by International Bible Society.
Scripture marked NLT is taken from the *Holy Bible*, New Living Translation, copyright 1996. Used by permission of Tyndale House Publishers, Inc., Wheaton, IL 60189. All rights reserved.
Scripture marked NCV is taken from THE HOLY BIBLE, New Century Version, copyright 1987, 1988, 1991 by Word Publishing, Dallas, Texas 75039. Used by permission.
Scripture marked KJV is from the King James Version of the Bible.
Scripture marked AMP is from the Amplified Bible. Old Testament copyright 1965, 1987 by the Zondervan Corporation. The Amplified New Testament copyright 1954, 1958, 1987 by the Lockman Foundation. Used by permission.
Scripture marked TEV is from Today's English Version of the New Testament. Copyright American Bible Society 1966, 1971. Used by permission.
Scripture marked NAB is from THE NEW AMERICAN BIBLE. Copyright Catholic Publishers, Inc., 1978, a Division of Thomas Nelson, Inc.

Publisher's Cataloging-in-Publication
(Provided by Quality Books, Inc.)

My roots go back to Loving : and other stories from
   Year of the family / Becky Cerling Powers, editor.
   -- 1st ed.
   p. cm.
   Includes index.
   LCCN: 99-74586
   ISBN: 0-9672134-1-X

   1. Spiritual life. 2. Family--Anecdotes.
I. Powers, Becky Cerling. II. El Paso times
(El Paso, Tex. : 1921)

BL624.M9 1999   158.1'28
                             QB199-992

Psalm 78: 4–8 (NLT)

We will not hide these truths from our children
 but will tell the next generation
 about the glorious deeds of the LORD.
We will tell of his power
 and the mighty miracles he did.
For he issued his decree to Jacob;
 he gave his law to Israel.
He commanded our ancestors
 to teach them to their children,
 so the next generation might know them
 – even children not yet born –
 that they in turn might teach their children.
So each generation can set its hope anew on God,
 remembering his glorious miracles
 and obeying his commands.

*This book is dedicated to our children and
our children's children.*

Contents

Foreword *Don Flores, Editor of the* El Paso Times	xi
Acknowledgments	xiii
The story behind these stories *Becky Cerling Powers*	1
Focusing on the good stuff *Joe Herman*	5
Saving Butterscotch *Karen M. Pickett Ward*	8
Chocolate pie mistake *Katherine Blake Markel*	10
Mama's prayers *Ruben Fierro as told to María Luisa Navarro*	12
Giving comfort *Jennifer Cummings*	14
My roots go back to Loving *Daniel Martinez*	16
Praying for a little brother *Herb Mims*	19
Lost and found cousins *Paula Kortkamp Harvie*	21
Start the day with love *Laura Jane Cerling*	23
Growing up in an orphanage *Mary Ann Herman*	25
The family secret *Peter Bulthuis*	28
One border, two families *Graciela Westeen as told to Becky Cerling Powers*	31

Calling Pepsi *Jennifer Cummings*   34

Rescuing my family from a battlefield   37
   Néaouguen Nodjimbadem
   as told to Becky Cerling Powers

Teaching school during war time,   41
   Néaouguen Nodjimbadem
   as told to Becky Cerling Powers

Practical jokes *Debbie Acton*   44
   as told to Becky Cerling Powers

Neighborly love *Dianne Roisen*   46

Miracle baby *Paula Kortkamp Harvie*   48

The family I needed *Noel Hart*   51

Turning 50 *Jennifer Cummings*   53

Praying for rain *Annette Horton Herrington*   55

Rescuing Joash *Laura Jane Cerling*   58

Learning at home *Matthew Powers*   60

Aunt Virginia *Jennifer Cummings*   63

Susan's monkey *Peter Bulthuis*   66

The mysterious patient *Paula Kortkamp Harvie*   69

Catching alcoholism *Bill Schlondrop*   72

Recovery from abortion *Rosie Chavarría Jones*   75
   as told to Becky Cerling Powers

Grandma thinks fast *Jennifer Cummings*	80
Dreaming of Anita Jo *Paula Kortkamp Harvie*	82
Early lessons pay off *Francis Diaz*	85
The church is family *Néaouguen Nodjimbadem* *as told to Becky Cerling Powers*	88
Psalm 91: antidote to insomnia *Paula Kortkamp Harvie*	91
My two dads *Janimarie Rowe* *as told to Becky Cerling Powers*	93
Mom's mouthwash *Virginia Payne Steely*	98
Susie's first funeral *Jennifer Cummings*	100
Home schooling chaos *Becky Cerling Powers*	102
Glad I listened *Laura Jane Cerling*	105
Grandma's Christmas in July *Zula McKenzie*	108
Faith vs. fear *Paula Kortkamp Harvie*	111
Ruth's double love story *retold by Maria Luisa Navarro*	114
A welcome for Kenny *Kathryn Knight-Chapman*	118
The loyalty of the orphans *Becky Cerling Powers*	121
The interrogation of Rosebud and Mama *Becky Cerling Powers*	124

Brotherly love *Sylvia R. Candelaria*   128

Smelling the flowers *Laura Jane Cerling*   130

A father's love *Guy Jones*   132

Back-up parents *Janet Allen*   134

Being a real friend *Kassie Yvonne Roden*   137

Forgiving Grandmother *Danielle McGill Hinesly*   139

God's therapy for families *Laura Jane Cerling*   142

Teagan's operation *Mary Ann Herman*   145

Refugees wandering *Laura Jane Cerling*   148

Dan's tree *Mary Ann Herman*   152

Foster grandparent *Jennifer Cummings*   154

Give me a perfect child, Lord *Janet M. Crowe*   157

Deciding to adopt *Vicky Clingermayer*   160

Lofty pine *Paula Kortkamp Harvie*   165

Index of Writers and Storytellers   168

Index of Values   171

About the Editor and Authors   175

Foreword

These stories first appeared in a series of daily columns published in *The El Paso Times* under the title, "1998: Year of the Family." The column was a follow up to "1997: Year of the Bible," sponsored by El Paso for Jesus, an organization of about 100 churches and pastors from many denominations in our city. Local churches wanted to encourage people in the city to read through the New Testament in 1997. Barney Field, director of El Paso for Jesus, persuaded our newspaper to publish a daily excerpt from the New Testament as part of that effort.

We agreed to that first project because El Paso is a strongly religious city, and we wanted to strengthen our religious coverage. That project was successful for our paper. It created great opportunities as the year unfolded to talk about differences among religions. When the Bible talked about an issue, readers from other persuasions would argue, "That's not in our religion." Then we used our religion coverage to talk about those differences. As a result, our readership in the features section increased and our religion coverage improved.

Around September of 1997, when that project was still going on, Barney Field came around to my office and said, "We've got another idea. How about another column for '1998: Year of the Family'?" We wanted to make a strong commitment to El Paso youth, and he was persuasive that this would help us do that. He pledged that he would find an army of folk to make it happen, so we committed to it.

Once again, it was a very successful year. The stories in the "1998: Year of the Family" column provided a nice hook to get good daily readership in our features section. There was a wonderful response from the community. Readers' response was universally positive. People said they liked that feature in our newspaper, and I did not hear one negative comment. The pieces were well thought out and there was continuity to the series. Folks like consistency in their lives, and our readers knew that every day there would be at least something in our newspaper that they could look forward to reading, something connected with their families and a religious aspect of family life. It was a quality column.

Don Flores, Editor, *El Paso Times*

Acknowledgments

Although I can't list everyone who helped to make this book possible, I would like to mention a few. My patient husband Dennis tops the list. Meeting the daily deadlines for the "1998: Year of the Family" column in *The El Paso Times*, from which these stories were chosen, took over my schedule for over a year. I could not have managed it without his full support.

The El Paso Writers' League, led by president Bill Schlondrop, made it possible to jump start the "Year of the Family" project. The *El Paso Times* staff was cooperative and patient. In particular I thank editor Don Flores for letting us try this community writing experiment, as well as Dan Williams, Paula Monarez Diaz, and Laurie Müller for their great attitudes and practical support.

Susan Anchondo and Mary Ann Herman recruited most of the writers, and Mary Ann was my right arm, dealing with uncountable details. Randy Limbird gave our writers an excellent writing workshop on conducting interviews. Barney Field, director of El Paso for Jesus, devised the basic format that followed the stories: quotation, model prayer, family resource. Without the encouragement and support of my prayer partners, Vicky Clingermayer and Karen Ward, I would never have started this project. In addition, Sharon Withers and Laurie Huffman encouraged Intercessors for Jesus International to pray in stories, strength, and supplies.

Pastor Clark Peters located family resources and answered theological questions that came up. Graciela and Ken Westeen, co-owners of Upper Valley Press, not only told her family's story within these pages but made resources available to help with typesetting.

Becky Cerling Powers, Editor

The story behind these stories

by Becky Cerling Powers

"Becky, WHERE do you get these stories?" one of the newspaper staff asked one day when I stopped by the *El Paso Times* news room to drop off a batch of "Year of the Family" columns.

"They drop out of heaven and land in my computer," I said. And I meant it.

As coordinator and editor for the "Year of the Family" writing project, I got used to being amazed by the stories that passed through my home computer on their way to the newspaper. Not just the stories, but the variety surprised me—humorous incidents, nail-biting drama, crystalline moments of insight, tender tributes, retold Bible stories, little-known gems from history.

The "Year of the Family" column was the brain child of a task force of pastors and civic leaders who came together to figure out ways for El Paso churches to work with civic leaders to help the city. After compiling an overwhelming list of problems facing El Paso (broken homes, addictions, domestic violence, weapons in schools, etc.), one pastor commented that the heart of our city's problems is people's value systems. "Actions are values made visible," he said. In other words, what people do shows what their values are.

So the task force decided to try to encourage the development of values that build up families. They sent Barney Field, Director of El Paso for Jesus, to ask Don Flores, Editor of the *El Paso Times,* to donate space for a daily column to help meet this purpose.

When Mr. Flores agreed, the task force asked me to volunteer to coordinate the project. I thought they were crazy: 365 columns? With volunteer, not-yet-recruited writers? After friends prayed with me about it, though, the El Paso Writers' League enthusiastically agreed to participate if I took on the responsibility. With their support, we began.

Each column told a story, followed by "Food for thought" (thought-stimulating comments), "Worth repeating" (a related quotation), "Today's prayer" (a model prayer that readers could pray in response to the story idea) and "Family resource" (a local agency or a book, video, or audio tape related to the story), as appropriate.

For me, the project became not only an adventure in mentoring writers and editing their stories, but an adventure in prayer. To give one recurring example, I often faced a deadline with an insufficient supply of stories—14 columns due in five days, for example, with only five columns in hand. I learned that instead of worrying, or complaining, I needed to follow Christ's example when he fed the 5,000—look at what I had, thank my heavenly Father for each story in that supply, then watch him increase it.

Time after time, as I gave thanks for what we had, our supply of stories began to multiply. Articles started showing up by e-mail, snail mail, and the fax machine. Individual stories sometimes multiplied into two, three,

The story behind these stories

or even four columns. Someone would send in a story that was too long and complicated to fit our space requirements. I would contact the writer and suggest ways for him or her to turn it into a two- or three-part continuing story. A number of the longer stories in this book, like "Ruth's double love story" by María Luisa Navarro (page 114), were originally published in the *El Paso Times* over several days as multi-part stories.

Columns started turning up in odd places, too, when we needed them. We discovered usable material in letters, speeches, sermons, old files, and newsletters. It was merely a matter of recognizing a story's potential and revising it to fit the requirements of the column.

After columns began appearing in the newspaper, more people became interested in writing for it. "Year of the Family" became a major community effort. Altogether, 80 people wrote the daily columns. Another 15 people told their stories to a writer for publication.

As the year progressed, people began to notice that stories in the column seemed to be directly commenting on issues raised in that same day's feature columns, editorials, or news reports. There was no way we could have planned this.

Probably the most dramatic example occurred the day the *El Paso Times* reported the tragic story of a mother and her two young daughters who died when their car was crushed between two semi-trucks in a highway construction-related accident. The news story described the shock and grief of members of the local church in which the family had been active. That day's "Year of the Family" story dealt with the question, "Why does God allow good, God-fearing people to die too young?" The writer described how a dream had helped her resolve her spiritual struggle when her college friend died in a car accident.

One of the many people who noticed that coincidence was the grandmother of the 12-year-old best friend of one of the children who died in the accident headlining that day's news. She cut out the column and shared it with her granddaughter, to comfort her. You can read that same column on page 82.

And so the stories that writers told for "Year of the Family" wove themselves into the family stories of readers and brought forth new stories.

For me, this tale of a grandmother comforting her grieving grandchild with a story from "Year of the Family" captured our hope for the daily column. As editor, I looked for stories that could encourage and strengthen families, stories that could be read by and shared with people of many ages, and stories that could provide natural ways to introduce and talk about spiritual issues and important values.

Some readers may be disappointed because their favorite story was not included. The "Year of Family" column produced a wealth of wonderful stories, and more collections are planned.

As people from other communities read these stories, we hope they will be inspired to do what El Paso did. We plan to publish two companion books to encourage that process: a manual for those interested in carrying out a "Year of the Family" project in their communities, and a writing guide for all ages based on this collection. Also, I have added stories behind some of the stories to prove that the supply of family-building, faith-based stories is limited only by our ability to recognize and express them. Our families and communities are wiser and better when we share them.

Focusing on the good stuff

by Joe Herman

    I'll never forget the time I hit a grand slam with my dad.
    I loved playing baseball as a kid. I always felt extra special when my dad came to the games. One game and one day were particularly memorable. It was Father's Day. I was in the starting lineup, and it was time to show off. Everything was perfect. Maybe I would go 3 for 3; maybe 2 for 3, or maybe hit a home run and maybe, just maybe, a home run with the bases loaded—a grand slam!
    But my first two times at bat, I struck out: 0 for 2. I was worried. Would I get another chance to redeem myself?
    I did. When I came up to bat the third time, my teammates were on base. It was my chance to get a hit and drive in those runs. But...strike one...strike two...then—a hitter always knows when he makes good contact. In that split second, a hitter knows it's going to

be a hit. A hitter also knows a split second later when it's a pop out...in the infield.

It was an extra high pop out. And it was the third out, too. I had failed to get a hit, had failed to drive the runners in, had gone 0 for 3, and had failed in front of my dad. As I headed to the bench, the players were saying, "Boy, what a major league pop out!"

It was a struggle, but I had to play the infield the next inning. I felt terrible and couldn't think about anything but the strike outs and the pop out and a perfect day, gone wrong. I was playing third base, wishing I could have another chance and not paying much attention, when the other team's best hitter came to bat.

He hit the ball hard, and on one or two hops it came toward me. It seemed like a rocket approaching. The ball came so fast to my right, I didn't have time to catch the ball in my glove. So I caught it in my bare hand. Ouch!

Coach always said, "Throw to first!" As I started to throw, I lost feeling in my hand and started to drop the ball. So I brought up my hand with the glove to keep the ball from touching the ground. Then I noticed the runner from second coming toward me. I tagged the runner out as he slid into me.

It must have looked good, because everyone congratulated me, even the other team's coaches.

The game ended. I'm not sure who won or lost. I remember getting ribbed about the "major league pop out" and accolades about "that play at third base." My only concern was what Dad would say—no home run, no double, no hits.

I'll always remember exactly what he said in the car on the way home: "That was a great play at third base."

I said, "Thanks."

Dad made no mention of anything except the play at third base. I felt relieved and proud. Dad saw the good thing I did. That day, I felt I had hit a grand slam with my dad.

Today, 30 years later, my dad has continued to overlook the strike outs and compliment me instead on the "good things."

Today, I still love baseball and my dad...and respect third basemen. Ouch!

Worth repeating: The Bible says, *"...Fix your thoughts on what is true and honorable and right. Think about things that are pure and lovely and admirable. Think about things that are excellent and worthy of praise"* (Phil. 4:8 NLT).

Today's prayer: *"Dear God, I'm sorry for focusing on negative things. Help me to look for something positive in hard situations and find something good in other people. From now on I choose to think on things that are lovely and true. Amen."*

 The story behind this story:

I don't know if our readers realized it, but Joe's father, Don Herman, was "1998: Year of the Family's" Champion Recipient of Tributes. It began when writer Mary Ann Herman told her adult children that "Year of the Family" was hoping to publish two or three weeks worth of stories and tributes to fathers in June. So several of the Herman clan wrote tributes to Don. Joe wrote two tributes, and his brother, Daniel, and sister-in-law, Lori, each wrote one as well. We published two in June close to Father's Day, and the others (which missed the deadline for Father's Day) later in the summer. The Herman family had a lot of fun surprising Don with their string of tributes. - ed.

Saving Butterscotch

by Karen M. Pickett Ward

"Mom, come look!" our 3-year-old, Andrew, called in a soft, awed voice. It was a hot summer day, not long after our family moved out of the city onto the beautiful desert mesa. And I was so glad I went to look right away! For there on the patio lay a coiled rattlesnake, preparing to strike our curious kitten.

Andrew didn't understand the danger. He thought this was another fresh experience for him to enjoy in his new desert home. I yelled and grabbed him and ran back into the house.

Our other two children quickly came to the patio door to see what the commotion was about. We all stood at the sliding glass door watching the stand-off between our kitty and the rattlesnake.

"Jesus, save our kitty!" the children pleaded, between cries of "No, Butterscotch, come inside!"

Without asking permission (I would have said "NO!"), our 11-year-old son, Matthew, took action. He quickly stepped onto the patio, swooped up the kitten in his arms—just inches away from the rattler—and ran back toward the house. With a sigh of relief, he slipped inside.

Then Matthew, whose father has taught him gun safety and marksmanship, shot the rattlesnake with his dad's shotgun from the safety of our kitchen window.

Worth repeating: The Bible says, *"There is no fear in love. But perfect love drives out fear, because fear has to do with punishment. The one who fears is not made perfect in love"* (1 John 4:18).

Food for thought: When someone we love is at risk, we can act in totally selfless ways, like Matthew did when he saved his cat. Jesus did that when he died to rescue us.

Today's prayer: *"Dear God, show us how to love each other in fearless and unselfish ways. Amen."*

Chocolate pie mistake

by Katherine Blake Markel

The clock by the bed said 6:02 a.m. I rushed toward the big farm kitchen, an eager 13-year-old hoping to be helpful. Heavenly aromas wafted through the house, testifying that Mrs. Barton had been baking pies since 4 a.m.

It was the week of harvest on the Bartons' vast Kansas farm. My good friend Shirley Barton and her parents had invited me to spend two weeks in the country with them, sharing in the adventure and hard work of threshing time.

During harvesting, the neighbors came to help Mr. Barton and his son work in the fields cutting and threshing wheat. The Barton men would then go to the neighbor's farm to help them in turn. Shirley and I were supposed to help Mrs. Barton serve the hungry threshers at a huge noon luncheon. We spent days preparing for that meal.

Finally the morning of the big event dawned. In the kitchen, I spent a few moments at my favorite window seat. Then I turned from the window to the kitchen table, which was laden with five different kinds of beautiful pies.

But what was this?? Chocolate pie filling was sliding down my leg and onto my socks. My hands dripped chocolate. I had sat in, and rested my hands in, three chocolate cream pies that were cooling on the window sill.

Horrified, I jumped away from the window seat expecting a sharp scolding from my friend's mother. What a stupid mistake I had made! My heart pounded and my eyes burned with tears of embarrassment. How could I face the family and all those threshers, and especially Mrs. Barton, after she had worked so hard on those pies?

Somehow Mrs. Barton kept her cool in that hot kitchen on that busy day. With calm dignity, she reassured me and relieved my panic. Then we cleaned up the mess. The threshers had to smile in spite of themselves at noon when they heard why they weren't being served any of their favorite chocolate pie.

I myself never forgot the gentle kindness of my friend's mother. In my heart I resolved to be just like Mrs. Barton, to forgive others for their mistakes the way she forgave me that summer morning.

Food for thought: Mrs. Barton realized that I needed reassurance instead of a scolding after my mistake. Why was she able to respond thoughtfully and appropriately instead of blowing up?

Worth Repeating: *"And be kind to one another, tenderhearted, forgiving one another, just as God in Christ also forgave you"* (Eph. 4:32 NKJ).

Today's Prayer: *"Thank you, Lord, for people who have been kind and forgiving to me even though I have made some bad mistakes. Help me to remember to forgive others when they disappoint me. Thank you for Your divine forgiveness. Amen."*

Mama's prayers

by Ruben Fierro
as told to María Luisa Navarro

Although Mama is no longer on this earth, I remember her with deep love and the greatest of respect.

I was born in El Paso 60 years ago, but to make ends meet, Mama courageously made the move to Los Angeles with me, a few dollars, and great faith in her God.

Our first "home" in East Los Angeles was in the roughest part of town called *El Ollo* (The Hole), so named because the shacks were in the middle of a dump. Mama got a job as a seamstress in a factory, and although she worked from 40 to 60 hours a week, she only earned $12 a week.

By the time I was 10 years old, I had various odd jobs—selling newspapers, carrying grocery bags for little *viejitas*, and shining shoes. Mama never asked me to get those jobs—in fact, it probably broke her heart. But I just desperately wanted to see my mama get freed up a little.

Mama's prayers

Mama always had a song on her lips, no matter what the circumstance, and there was always a lot of love that poured out from her. She was also the most generous person I knew. When she'd get paid, she'd send me to the *tiendita* to change a dollar bill into four quarters. She always had them handy for the Chavezes or Gonzalezes or whoever was in need, and she'd send me over there with quarters in a little handkerchief.

The thing about Mama that stands out most in my mind, though, is that she had great faith and always prayed for me. You see, for 27 years I was an alcoholic and drug addict. Her friends and relatives told her that I would end up in San Quentin or dead on the street, but Mama never gave up on me or on the God who had the power to save me.

Mama always believed in her heart that I would get clean and live for the Lord. I am grateful today to be able to say that for over 20 years now, I've been doing just that!

Food for thought: A mother's prayers are powerful.

Worth repeating: *"(Love) always protects, always trusts, always hopes, always perseveres"* (1 Cor. 13:7).

Today's prayer: *"Lord, I thank You for those in my life who have never given up on me. Show me daily how to love and respect them. Amen."*

Giving comfort

by Jennifer Cummings

How do you give comfort to someone whose loved one has died?

Crushing weight on my chest made breathing nearly impossible. Sharp pains in my left arm signaled a heart attack. Gushing tears deformed the tissues of my eyes and face. Water would not pass the constriction in my throat.

My mind kept repeating the awful message, "We're sorry, Mrs. Olson, your husband is dead." My heart was broken. Was there anything that anyone could do to comfort me? Certainly . . .

Hold me while I sob. Greg and Sharon arrived to hold me as I sobbed. On my knees, I hugged son Sean as he beat the living room floor with his fists. My sisters traveled a thousand miles before nightfall to be at my side. Pastor Bill cut short a personal trip and returned home from Phoenix. Son Dan greeted me with tears and a hug at the airport.

Help with tasks that need to be done. Lee located my husband's car and brought it safely home.

Sharon accompanied son Sean as he shared our tragic news with his high school friends. Rita drove to the airport to pick up arriving family members. Rosemary answered the constantly ringing telephone.

Express sympathy. Friends and neighbors brought food. Co-workers sent flowers. A thousand caring people delivered hugs, cards of sympathy, and words of encouragement. A woman that I had never met wrote a note telling about a kind deed my husband had done for her.

Provide support during transition to life without the loved one. After the busyness of the funeral, Phyllis invited me to dinner, Tom offered lawn care, Irma shared a book on grief, and all of my family kept their arms around us. Son Dan showed his care: "I don't need that much money, Mom."

Respect the memories. It is now 12 years later. I am happily remarried. The memories still bring tears, but I have been blessed with an understanding husband who respects my past and wipes away my tears.

Yes, there are a lot of things that people can do to offer comfort to the bereaved.

Food for thought: What you say to a grieving person is not as important as letting the grieving person know that you care.

Worth repeating: Friends and family give strength. *"If one falls down, his friend can help him up. But pity the man who falls and has no one to help him up!"* (Eccl. 4:10).

Today's prayer: *"Dear God, thank You for giving us family and friends to help us up when we are down. Let us be good helpers when it is our turn to offer comfort to others. Amen."*

My roots go back to Loving

by Daniel Martinez

My roots go back to Loving. That's where my grandparents lived—Loving, New Mexico. It's a small town, but it was a big place in my life.

When my grandparents started life together, times were tough. Bolito and Bolita, as I've called them since I could talk, were happy the day Bolito got a job sweeping the floor at the nearby potash refinery. Over the years he learned to read and write and also to speak English. His company rewarded his efforts by increasing his responsibilities and wages continuously. He showed his gratitude with 40 years of devoted service until his retirement.

Bolita worked hard, too, waking up at 4 a.m. to make fresh tortillas so she could send Bolito off to work with a good breakfast and a well-packed lunch. I remember that metal lunch box. Everyday I would wait for Bolito to get home to see if there was anything left inside it for me to eat, and every day he made sure there was.

Together Bolito and Bolita raised three daughters, two sons, and two adopted grandchildren. Both my parents worked, so my grandparents took care of me, too. They loved me—mind, body, and soul.

Sometimes I attended Mass at the Catholic church with Bolito. No matter how large the crowd, the large building was always hushed. Latin words, flickering candles, flowing robes, stained glass, the solemn dignity of the Mass, and the sweet music of the unseen choir gave me a sense of the ancient, mysterious beauty of God.

Sometimes I went with Bolita to the nearby Assembly of God church. People talked and laughed before the service, and then they began almost non-stop singing, broken now and then by an impassioned sermon, punctuated with hallelujahs and amens. There was a sense of closeness to God here and now!

Bolita once told me that God was not in a building, but in your heart. Going to church or being "religious" was not God. God is Love, and love is forgiving others as many times as it takes. That was the greatest thing she had learned, she said, and the thing she would change about her younger days.

Last year, Bolita passed away. Whenever we speak of her, tears well up in Bolito's eyes. They were married 66 years. Bolito says that, although he is tired, he is unready to die. Life is precious. He is 88.

This is why my roots are in Loving, New Mexico. My grandparents showed me what is truly important in life. Looking at their lives, I can see that the joy of life is LOVE: simple, undemanding, all-giving, pure love.

Everyone should have roots in Loving.

Worth repeating: *"From everlasting to everlasting the LORD's love is with those who fear him, and his righteousness with their children's children—with those who* keep his covenant and remember to obey his precepts" (Psalm 103:17–18).

Today's prayer: *"Thank you, Lord, for this promise that Your love will keep our family going through the generations. Help me to do my part of the bargain, keeping Your standards and teaching my children and grandchildren what You expect of our family. Amen."*

📖 **The story behind this story:**

The "Year of the Family" column gave many families a great gift: the opportunity to honor their loved ones and express appreciation publicly through family stories. Bolito cried when he read his grandson's tribute to him in the newspaper. He died not long afterward, and when his family went through his personal effects, they discovered a copy of this column in his wallet. - ed.

Praying for a little brother

by Herb Mims

"Why don't I have a brother or sister?" our 3-year-old asked us.

We knew our son could not understand the medical complications we were facing. We told him that God had only given us one child, but that he could pray for a younger brother or sister. Later, we learned that when he attended church with other preschoolers, he would pray for a brother or sister.

For several years my wife and I attempted to increase our family. She had a tubal pregnancy—a life-threatening situation—and emergency surgery. Then there were tests and more tests. One procedure showed that her fallopian tubes were fiber-filled. An endoscopic surgery would provide only slight hope.

We became discouraged. We had prayed for a second child, but after so long our faith had become weak. However, that was untrue for our son. As a 4 year old, a 5 year old, a 6 year old, he prayed regularly for a sibling. He never gave up his hope. Then, just after his seventh birthday, we received the news—my wife was pregnant.

It was exciting for our family to follow the development and birth of a child. Our greatest excitement, however, was a new understanding of the value of prayer. Our son's prayers reminded my wife and me that prayer is important, and that prayer will be answered. God may not answer when we expect, or even how we expect, but he will answer.

Food for thought: The faith of a preschool boy taught us again that faith is vital in prayer. We must not give up when we pray. Because we do not feel God's presence, or because we do not receive an answer immediately, does not mean he is not listening. God accepts the smallest faith, and hears the shortest prayer. Let the faith of a small child lead you to a renewed commitment to prayer. Prayer will not only change circumstances, it will change you.

Worth repeating: Jesus said, *"Have faith in God. Listen to me! You can pray for anything, and if you believe, you will have it"* (Mark 11:22,24 NLT).

Today's prayer: *"Heavenly Father, thank You for inviting me to come to You with all my needs. Thank You for Your promise to answer prayer when I ask believing in Your power to answer. And thank You that prayer does indeed change things. Amen."*

Lost and found cousins

by Paula Kortkamp Harvie

Growing up in Illinois as an only child, I looked forward to holidays when my cousins from Iowa came to visit. Nancy and Mary were fun. We loved to play hide-and-go-seek in my grandparents' creaky old house and scare ourselves with ridiculous spook stories. One memorable, snowy day we foolishly lay under a sun lamp for a winter tan and ended up with our faces burned and our eyes swollen shut. We got in trouble for that, but other adventures turned out better.

Then sadly, my cousins' parents divorced, and our good times together ended.

Grandma Kortkamp was distressed by the separation within the family. "Honey," she often said to me, "promise you will always keep in touch with Nancy and Mary." Solemnly I promised.

My cousins and I corresponded well into early adulthood, but then, as time went by, addresses and last names changed. Other priorities claimed our attention, and we lost contact. I often wondered about my cousins. I always felt a pang of remorse that I'd not kept my promise to Grandma. If only I had answered my cousins' last letters back in the 1970s, we wouldn't have lost touch. But now I didn't know how to find them.

Then in January 1997, my mother received a note postmarked from a town we'd never heard of. It was from Nancy. She and Mary had found Mother's address on the Internet and wanted to hear from us.

Thrilled, I immediately I sat down and wrote. How grateful I was that God was giving me a new opportunity to keep my childhood promise to Grandma. My cousins and I began communicating several times a week through e-mail, sometimes several times a day.

The last time we saw each other we were just children. Now we are mothers and grandmothers ourselves. It has been a great joy for us as adults to build a new relationship. And yes, we have even met for several reunions in Iowa. We treasure our moments together with a deeper realization of just how precious family relationships are.

Food for thought: Our grandmother invested countless hours praying for us, her grandchildren. Although she died 45 years ago, her prayers are still bearing fruit in our lives. She always prayed that Nancy, Mary, and I would have a close relationship so that we might encourage one another spiritually. After many decades that prayer is now being answered.

Worth repeating: *"The earnest prayer of a righteous person has great power and wonderful results"* (James 5:16 NLT).

Today's prayer: *"Dear Lord, thank You for the power of prayer. Help me to invest in my family's future by faithfully praying for each member. Thank You for answering our prayers in Your perfect way and in Your perfect timing. Amen."*

Start the day with love

by Laura Jane Cerling

I don't remember why I was upset that morning, but as my kindergartner went out the door, my scolding voice echoed in my ears. I watched the little figure trudge off on his way to kindergarten, and I saw his shoulders slump.

I thought I heard a voice, "Laura Jane, don't you EVER do that again! You are sending him off in discouragement to his world of school." I realized then that the sharp disapproval of my voice could color every event of his school day.

I do not know whether the voice I heard was the voice of my conscience, or if God spoke to me. But I felt severely rebuked, and I've never forgotten that morning. From that day on, I tried always to send my husband and children off in a good frame of mind. Their world of work or school with its problems, challenges, and disappointments would be handled more successfully if their day started well.

I'm sure there were times I forgot my new resolution, but I tried to keep it in mind every morning. The challenge increased later when that kindergartner grew and his teen years came. Our communication was often strained and almost stifled. During one such long period of time, I remember thinking with desperation, *I must send my son off on a positive note!*

So each morning as he went to leave, I followed him to the door, touched him lightly on the shoulder and said, "Have a good day!"

I don't know what it did for him, but it was good for me. I needed to be able to express my love and concern in a way that he could accept.

The payoff has been great. Our six children love and respect one another as well as us, their parents. There are many miles separating us, but the times we are together are happy and satisfying.

Food for thought:
"Then deem it not an idle thing
A pleasant word to speak
The face you wear, the thought you bring
A heart may heal or break." (J.G. Whittier)

Worth repeating: The Bible says, *"Anxiety in the heart of man causes depression, but a good word makes it glad"* (Prov. 12:25 NKJ).

Today's prayer: *"Lord, help me to think before I speak. May the words I say, and the way that I say them, be helpful and not harmful. Amen."*

Growing up in an orphanage

by Mary Ann Herman

"The boys were very upset with the nuns at our orphanage," Clara B. Little said as she described the big fire at Texas Store. "The store's owner had to get rid of everything, including huge bolts of yellow and pink flowered drapery fabric. It was during the Depression, and our seamstress nun saw it as a free gift of material that could be made into clothes for ALL the children."

That happened in the early 1930s. It was not unusual in those days for youngsters to live in an orphanage. Clara and her sister, Frances Endlich, were placed in an El Paso orphanage run by the Sisters of Charity of Incarnate Word after their father died.

"Our mother had to work and had no one to care for us at home," said Frances. "She visited us whenever possible. We had about eight to ten nuns taking care of us. They were good and loving, but firm in teaching us all the virtues, especially honesty and respect. When we were of high school age, we moved back with our mother."

Seeing to the needs of 85 children kept the Sisters of Charity busy. They fed, they clothed, they bathed, they washed, and they ironed. Then they nourished the youngsters' souls with gospel stories and the Ten Commandments. A typical day's activities included 6:30 a.m. Mass and classes, with breaks for three hearty meals and welcome snacks.

The nuns trained the older children to look after the younger ones. "The nuns showed us how to be protective of everyone, and we learned responsibility," the women said.

Even a holy nun could have a sense of humor, the women recalled. "There was always a big pile of clothes to patch," they said. "Sister Stephanie accidentally cut off the 'good leg' from a pair of long johns. She stared at her mistake and then laughed out loud at herself."

The orphanage raised fruits and vegetables, and the farmhand Tony tended two or three cows. "There was always freshly churned butter, thanks to Tony, and those fresh tomatoes were so good!" The women said, "Sometimes we'd sneak into the orchard and take the green apples."

"Christmas was special with a big tree," they said. "We'd get all dressed up because we knew there would be gifts for every child. Easter egg hunts were fun, too. On Sunday evenings we'd walk with the nuns, hold hands, and pick flowers. And we used to walk about a mile to the movies at Ysleta. If there was a scary movie, you could see about 20 of us leave the theater in fright."

"Because of abuse in some other child-care institutions, orphanages might have had a bad connotation," the women said. "But most orphanages, including ours, tried to keep families together with kindness and understanding."

Growing up in an orphanage

"I'll always have a warm spot in my heart for those nuns," said Clara, and Frances agreed with grateful thanks.

Worth repeating: *"Religion that God our Father accepts as pure and faultless is this: to look after orphans and widows in their distress and to keep oneself from being polluted by the world"* (James 1:27).

Today's prayer: *"Lord, help me to honor and express thanks for those who cared for me when I was small. Amen."*

📖 The story behind this story:

This story came to the *El Paso Times* thanks to Dawn Marie Caruthers. One day when Dawn Marie and I were talking about stories in the "Year of the Family" column, she said, "I have two elderly aunts who were raised by nuns in a Catholic orphanage right here in El Paso. They have very fond memories of growing up in the orphanage, and they tell all kinds of stories about it. You should talk to them." Dawn Marie checked with her aunts to see if they would be willing to tell their stories to a writer, and then Mary Ann Herman interviewed them to give El Paso this charming memoir. - ed.

The family secret

by Peter Bulthuis

It was the first week of school in Lynden, Washington, in September 1967. I was still trying to arrange things in my new counseling office when Anna walked in and sat down. After asking and being assured that what she told me would not be told to her mother or the teachers, she blurted out, "Mr. Bulthuis, I don't like my mother!"

"Well, I guess you're not the first girl to have negative feelings about her mother."

"But you don't understand! I really hate her!"

"You really hate her!"

"Maybe I don't hate her, but I don't really want to be around her. As soon as I graduate I'm getting married and we're going to move to Wisconsin where my boyfriend has relatives and I won't have to see her."

After ten minutes of sorting out what she really disliked about her mother, it came down to the fact that she resented her mother's making a certain remark every time she went out with her boyfriend, "Now you be careful!"

Anna added, "She even says it right in front of him!"

I suggested that she wait until a time when just the two of them would be together and that she tell her mother that this remark bothered her a lot.

Before school the next morning, she burst into my office. "I did what you said last night when my mom and I were doing dishes. I told her I didn't like her saying that. She said she had a good reason but didn't want to tell me. When I begged her to tell me, she told me this story that she has never told anyone since she immigrated from Holland."

"When her older sister was a teenager, she got pregnant. She said that my grandfather was a very stern, very proud man. He told his daughter that he wasn't going to let her disgrace him in front of the whole town, and he locked her upstairs in her bedroom. He had my grandmother take her food up there. He said he was going to take the baby to the city for adoption. Two weeks before the baby was to be born, my aunt committed suicide."

"Mr. Bulthuis, my poor mother has lived with this secret her whole life. I'm the only one she has told. I told her that she may keep saying that remark to me when I date, if it helps her."

The next spring, I asked Anna if she still planned to marry and move to Wisconsin. She said, "We're going to wait eight months and both earn some money before we get married. We decided that we do not want to move to Wisconsin. We're going to buy a mobile home and put it on my folks' farm because my mother and I are really close friends now!"

Worth repeating: *"Though good advice lies deep within a person's heart, the wise will draw it out"* (Prov. 20:5 NLT).

Today's prayer: *"Dear God, when my family hurts me, help me not to be angry but instead try to find out what is behind their words or behavior. Amen."*

 The story behind this story:
I first read this story in a book of memoirs that Peter Bulthuis originally wrote as a gift to his children, *Ka Mo Ter Wou*, which means "It is me, your father" in the language of the Tiv tribespeople of Nigeria. So many friends and relatives wanted copies of the book that Peter self-published it and sold it in a local bookstore in his home in Lynden, Washington. Peter's nephew, Ken Scholten, lives in El Paso and served on the committee that proposed the idea for the "Year of the Family" column. When we were looking for stories, Ken thought to show me a copy of his uncle's delightful memoir. I contacted Peter, who agreed to let us revise some of his stories for publication in the column. To order a copy of *Ka Mo Ter Wou*, write to Peter Bulthuis at 1710 Liberty St., Apt. 103, Lynden, WA 98264. - ed.

One border, two families

by Graciela Westeen
as told to Becky Cerling Powers

My parents raised two families, their own six children plus six of my cousins. My cousins had to stay on the Mexican side of the border because they were not American citizens. So it was complicated. My parents juggled two families on both sides of the border.

Dad was a farm worker, and Mother worked in a garment factory. My mom was from New Mexico, and Dad became a naturalized citizen through her after they married. They had six children, half born here and half born in Mexico. By the time my father's brother died, my parents had paid for a house in Juárez, Mexico, across the river from El Paso, Texas.

My aunt in Juárez was left with six children, about ages 5 to 15. She struggled for a couple of years, but she became emotionally unstable and had to be hospitalized. After a few years, she died, too.

My mom and dad put the two families together— 12 kids. Mother made much better wages in El Paso so she lived in an apartment in El Paso during the week and lived with us in Juárez on weekends. My dad kept an eye on us all. On Fridays, at the end of her work week, we'd sit and wait for Mother at the bridge on the U.S.-Mexico border. Then her work started all over again for the weekend, because she'd have to cook, clean house, and iron for the week.

My three boy cousins were rebellious. The oldest didn't want any part of us and left. The other two were younger teens who liked the Juárez night life.

My parents wanted us to better our lives. Sometimes some of us lived with Mother in the apartment and went to school in El Paso. We went back and forth, living in the two cities. Finally the El Paso school superintendent said we had to live here in order to attend school here.

By that time my oldest cousin had skipped out, and another boy cousin had died of tuberculosis. (A few years later the third boy cousin also died of tuberculosis.) By then my cousins were all teenagers, except for the littlest one. My two older siblings stayed in Juárez, and the rest of the family moved to El Paso. It was about 1954.

My parents continued to support both families, with two places to live, two of everything. Our family rented a tenement apartment in south El Paso. All the apartments shared outside sinks and outside bathrooms. We went to the community center in Armijo Park to take our showers.

The door to our apartment was next to the alley where the garbage dumpsters were. My mom said no matter where we lived, we had to be clean. So, weather permitting, every afternoon we had to clean up around the dumpsters. She said we wouldn't live there forever, and we didn't. Eventually my parents bought a house in central El Paso, and we got away from the dumpsters.

My three girl cousins are all legal American citizens now. They went through the whole long process of immigration and naturalization. Two of them married and live in Spokane, Washington. The youngest, Maria Luisa, is a nun who has lived all over the United States. I got my high school education, and so did two of my sisters. My husband and I now own Upper Valley Press in Canutillo, Texas.

My mom was always disappointed that she didn't save those young men from going wayward. But if I was in her shoes, I couldn't do more. I think she did the best she could with what she had.

Food for thought: The Bible clearly teaches that adults are responsible to provide for their families. This can be difficult, but with God's help, it is possible.

Worth repeating: The Apostle Paul taught, *"If anyone does not provide for his relatives, and especially for his immediate family, he has denied the faith and is worse than an unbeliever"* (1 Tim. 5:8).

Today's prayer: *"Loving God, please give me the faith and strength to fulfill my responsibilities to my family today. Amen."*

 The story behind this story:

Wonderful stories can be found in all kinds of places, in every community. I first heard this moving story of family sacrifice about 10 years ago, while waiting on the photocopy machine in Graciela Westeen's print shop. It is a story unique to El Paso. It could have happened nowhere else in the United States. In 1998, when I was looking for material for the "Year of the Family" column, I remembered the story and asked Graciela to tell it to me again, this time for publication. - ed.

Calling Pepsi

by Jennifer Cummings

"Jennifer, I need you! Come now!" my brother called from outside. I knew the problem immediately and was pleased to have my older brother coming to me for help.

Our family farm was in west-central Minnesota. At 15, I had two cows of my own. The first was named Seven-up. She had a white marking resembling the shape of a seven on her forehead. Seven-up had no particular talents other than grazing, producing milk, and being the mother of Pepsi.

But Pepsi? That was another story. She was special.

When Pepsi was a small calf, we bonded. I loved her. She loved me. Whenever I fed her, I whistled and she came running to me. Sometimes, just wanting to pet her, I went to her pen and whistled. Pepsi came and nuzzled me as I petted her. Our affection for each other remained strong and Pepsi never forgot my whistle signal for her to come.

For those who have not spent time on a farm, cows are kept in fenced-in pastures where they wander about and graze. Cows tend to hang out together; where one goes, the others follow.

On this particular day when my brother was so urgently calling for me to come, one of our cows had found (or created) a hole in the fence surrounding the pasture. Within a short time our family's entire herd of dairy cows was outside of the fence.

They headed to a neighbor's corn field. The more my brother ran after and yelled at the cows, the faster they ran, scattering in all directions, doing more and more damage to the tender young corn plants. Finally my brother stopped. He had to get his little sister's help.

I hurried from the house and followed my brother to the neighbor's corn field. I whistled. Pepsi stopped, lifted her ears, and turned around. I whistled again. Pepsi came. Remember that cows hang out together ... well, the rest of the cows soon followed after Pepsi. Pepsi, my brother, and I walked home to our family pasture, and the other cows followed.

I was happy. I could depend on Pepsi to come when I whistled. She saved my brother and me a lot of running to round up the scattered cows. She saved most of the neighbor's corn field. And, I was secretly pleased that I could do something that my brother couldn't. Yes, I was happy that I could depend on my cow.

Food for thought: We value things in life we can depend on — cars, friends, family, pets. When someone or something is dependable, it has greater value, just as Pepsi had more value to me than Seven-Up. What are some ways that we can become more dependable sons or daughters or friends?

Worth repeating: God promises that we can depend on him, *"Never will I leave you; never will I forsake you"* (Hebrews 13:5).

Today's prayer: *"Dear God, I know that it is important to be dependable. I do pretty well, but sometimes it seems too difficult, complicated, or inconvenient. That's when I need Your help so that I do not disappoint my parents, my friends, or You, God. Amen."*

 📖 **The story behind this story:**
  Part of the fun of working with the "Year of the Family" column was discovering talented, but unpublished writers. Jennifer Cummings is a retired accountant who learned about the "Year of the Family" writing project through the El Paso Writers' League. She had published only one article before writing for this project, but she became one of our more prolific writers, publishing 26 columns altogether. "Writing for 'Year of the Family' was very pleasurable for me," Jennifer commented at the end of the project. "I experienced growth in my writing skills with Becky's coaching. My personal values were clarified and strengthened through the process of writing a story with a message for others. And, I found my writing niche—short, non-fiction pieces."
- ed.

Rescuing my family from a battlefield

by Néaouguen Nodjimbadem
as told to Becky Cerling Powers

When civil war erupted in Chad in February 1979, I was 29 years old, teaching in a Christian high school in the capitol city, N'Djamena. The central city was being bombed, and we could hear gunfire all day, all night. There were dead bodies all over the neighborhood.

We had to shut the school down, and the students and teachers had to flee for their lives. For me, fleeing was complicated because I had so many in my extended family to help move out.

At that time in Chad, not many children had the opportunity to go to high school because all the secondary schools were only in the big cities. Children from villages and small towns, like my younger siblings, had to leave their parents and live in the city with relatives. So I had my two brothers, my sister, and my cousins with me.

One of my younger brothers was in the hospital at the time. He had a narrow escape. On Sunday he had exploratory surgery followed by an appendectomy. Monday morning the war started, and his part of the hospital building caught fire when a bomb exploded. He was transferred to the part of the building that wasn't burned, but it was four days before we first knew that he was alive.

My older sister's situation was bad, too. She had seven children, ranging in age from 2 to 17. Her husband was in Europe at that time, and the family lived a few yards away from the house of Hisseine Habré, the prime minister. Her kids, especially the youngest ones, were traumatized by the war because Habré's neighborhood was targeted by the regular army. The army even dropped bombs from airplanes.

For years a rebellion against the Chadian government had been simmering in the northern part of the country. Then Felix Malloum, the second president of Chad, signed a peace accord with Habré, leader of the rebellion, and named him prime minister. Habré still wanted the power, however, and with the help of French troops that were stationed in Chad, he started the civil war – a war that continues today, even though Habré himself is now in exile.

N'Djamena is divided into two parts. In the northern part live people who are originally from the Islamic northern tribes. In the southern part live people from the Christianized southern tribes. The civil war in Chad is ethnic, religious, and all those things together. So if you were from the wrong tribal background in the wrong part of the city, your life was in danger. It was not just a matter of avoiding soldiers in uniform. Anyone might shoot you. Some of my friends were shot before they got out of the city.

I could not sleep. What was happening to my sister and her children? What was happening to my brother and my aunt, who was staying with him in the hospital? With all the shooting, we could not travel to the hospital or to my sister's house to help the family or find out if they were still alive.

When the first cease fire was called four days after the fighting began, my sister just took the children and walked to my house, five miles away. It was so terrible for them. They left home empty handed, with only the clothes on their backs. My aunt was in the hospital with my brother, taking care of him. It was only five days after his surgery, but they also walked six to seven miles to my house. There was no way you could get a car.

When they all arrived safely, I was finally able to sleep for the first time in four days.

We called Missionary Aviation Fellowship (MAF) to ask for help for my brother. MAF said they had to fly to the south, and they agreed to save two places for that brother and my younger sister. The Red Cross helped us take them to the airport, and MAF flew them down to a southern hospital.

After several days we were able to pay for a truck to get the rest of the family out of the city. We packed light, bringing only what we could hold in our hands. Switching trucks two or three times on the way, we rode all the way to my parents' home in Moundou, 350 miles away, in the back of trucks, packed in with dozens of other refugees.

Unfortunately, when we reached Moundou, the fighting was going on there, too. (The story continues in "Teaching school during war time" on page 41.)

Worth repeating: *"I took my troubles to the LORD; I cried out to him, and he answered my prayer"* (Psalm 120:1 NLT).

Today's prayer: *"Thank You, God, for Your servants who risk their lives to help strangers who are in trouble. I pray that the people of Chad, and other countries in conflict, will be willing to take risks, too, to sit down and* *agree to bring justice for all and to come to peace with each other to unite the country. I pray as well for mercy for the families in nations at war who face danger today. Help them to cry out to You and experience Your deliverance. Amen."*

 The story behind this story:

In April 1998, Nodji (Néaouguen Nodjimbadem) learned that the simmering civil war in Chad had broken out again in Moundou, where his mother and siblings live. He began staying up until 2 a.m. to listen to news on short wave radio. He agonized over the reports of many casualties and kept trying to telephone his family, but he was unable to get through. Finally, a missionary friend told him by e-mail that his family members were still alive and well.

Nodji was anxious to publicize the need for prayer for Chad, so he set up a prayer meeting at First Baptist Church in El Paso. Afterward, we contacted Barney Field, Director of El Paso for Jesus for ideas to help Nodji get prayer for his people. Barney suggested that the "Year of the Family" column might provide a way to do that. "Why didn't I think of that?" I said.

So I sat down with Nodji and a tape recorder. Nodji told me many stories about his family and the suffering church in Chad. The stories published in this collection are just a sample. Through these stories, many El Pasoans learned about the plight of the people of Chad and their need for prayer.

"I know that a lot of people prayed for Chad," Nodji said. "I received a lot of phone calls after people started reading the articles, and people in my church talked to me, encouraged me, and prayed for me. Even people who were not from my church would meet me in town and say, 'Oh, are you the one who wrote the articles in the paper?' They said they prayed, too. That helped me a lot. For a while I was hearing from people every day."
- ed.

Teaching school during wartime

by Néaouguen Nodjimbadem
as told to Becky Cerling Powers

I was teaching in a Christian high school in N'Djamena, the capitol of Chad, when civil war erupted. I had a traumatic time getting my younger sister and two brothers out of the city, along with my aunt, cousins, older sister, and my sister's seven children.

We fled 350 miles south to my parents in our home town, Moundou, only to find that people were fighting there, too. Everything was shut down throughout the country. Soldiers were shooting civilians, raping the women, extorting food and money, and plundering the goods and property of fleeing refugees.

We completely lost the school term from February to November, but we thought it was important for the students to get their education even with war going on. We believed education would be the solution to end the war in Chad. If people are educated, we thought, then they can learn to sit down and talk about what is good for the country instead of just killing each other.

Because of the fighting still going on in N'Djamena, we transferred the school to a village down south. Then we had to call all our students back to open the school. We made announcements over the radio to try to contact them. They didn't all come back because of the whole situation. It was hard for parents to let their kids go away. But some came back, and we started the school.

All the teachers made sacrifices to keep the school going. The financial situation was hard. What little money we could collect every month, we divided among us. Each received the same amount. It was not that great, but we shared and made sacrifices to make it possible for the school to continue.

Many of the students had no one to take care of them and no money to pay for housing or food. So each of the teachers took care of two or three students. They lived with us, and we met their expenses. I had four kids with me, including my younger sister and brother. It was important for me to help those kids keep going in their education. I knew that without support, they would have to drop out.

I'm happy I did that for those kids. Today one of them is a high school teacher. Another one is married with children, and a third one is working as a telecommunications technician. I don't know the whereabouts of the fourth one.

The school is still in operation today. Eventually the church moved it back to N'Djamena. All their buildings were still there, although they were damaged. The roofs were all gone, and so were the doors, windows and all the equipment. The church rebuilt the school.

Worth repeating: *"All the believers were of one heart and mind, and they felt that what they owned was not their own; they shared everything they had"* (Acts 4:32 NLT).

Today's prayer: *"Dear God, thank You for sending a spirit of love and cooperation to this group of teachers and students so that they were able to work in harmony. Please work in the hearts of the Chadian people, and also in the hearts of those in other warring nations, so that they will be willing to cooperate with each other to restore order and to bring freedom of speech and freedom of religious belief to their country. Amen."*

Practical jokes

by Debbie Acton
as told to Becky Cerling Powers

One night before our teenage daughter left on a long trip, two of her friends snuck over to our house and set to work in the darkness to give her a send off surprise.

No, they didn't "fork" the yard. They didn't cover the trees and bushes with toilet paper, either. Instead they decorated our driveway with bright sidewalk chalk. They created a work of art, with a design that covered the entire driveway surface. It looked like a mural. All our neighbors came over to admire it the next morning, and I took a picture of it.

We have raised two daughters, so we've experienced the various fads of adolescence. One fad that has been around a long time is toilet papering people's property in the middle of the night. Fifteen years ago, teens did this to someone they disliked. Now they do it to their friends.

Once a group of our daughter's friends totally papered our house and yard during the night to "welcome" her home after a trip. The sprinklers came on, and it was a horrible wet mess. The whole family had to get out and clean up. Some of the paper in the tops of the trees took months to get out.

I thought, "What a way to come home – having to get out and clean up your yard first thing, with grumpy parents. This toilet paper ritual doesn't make sense. Isn't there a better way to show someone you like them?"

There is. The driveway mural idea was beautiful, like a gift. And I thought it was neat for the young kids in our court to see what the teens had done. It encouraged them to be more creative using sidewalk chalk themselves.

There was no extra work for us either. We didn't have to worry about the driveway, because the chalk wore off in a week.

Food for thought: The driveway artists showed respect for their friend's parents and respect for the family's property by choosing to use their hands to make a beautiful gift instead of using their hands to make a terrible mess. Which activity takes more creativity?

Worth repeating: The Bible says, *"So in everything, do to others what you would have them do to you, for this sums up the Law and the Prophets"* (Matt. 7:12).

Today's prayer: *"Dear God, teach me to show love through kind and thoughtful actions. Show me something I can do today."* Amen

Neighborly love

by Dianne Roisen

Although we were home now from the hospital, I hesitated going into the house. I knew our other three children (ages 7, 10, and 12) would rush at me, asking questions about their brother, Aaron. How badly was he hurt? Was he going to live?

My husband and I had spent all night at the hospital. Our 16-year-old son had been in a car accident with his friends. Two of them had died, and the doctor said he didn't know yet how badly Aaron was hurt. We prayed he would improve.

I took three deep cleansing breaths, somehow expecting the crisp December air to renew my body, replacing despair and weariness with hope and inner strength. Instead, it was the love and compassion of my friends and neighbors that renewed me.

When I entered the house, I found my children ladling soup from an unfamiliar kettle. On the counter next to it was a note saying:

Don't worry about fixing supper for the next six nights. Your neighbors will be taking care of you!

I sat down and wept tears of thankfulness.

In the days that followed, concerned friends dropped off more food. The six days of supper turned into sixteen. The children especially liked the desserts and free pizza certificates.

Having food prepared gave me and my husband extra time to spend at the hospital with our son and to be at home comforting and sharing our thoughts with the children. I shall never forget the December of 1996 and the compassion our friends showed us. I pray that God will bless them as he has blessed us with our son's complete recovery.

Worth repeating: The Bible says, *"Give, and it will be given to you. A good measure, pressed down, shaken together and running over, will be poured into your lap. For with the measure you use, it will be measured to you"* (Luke 6:38).

Food for thought: It takes a lot of time to plan meals and shop for groceries. Having to do all that work would have added extra stress to my husband and me when we were already trying to cope with our son's accident and injuries. Our friends and neighbors showed how much they cared by pitching in to help with meals.

Today's prayer: *"Dear God, when others are suffering and hurting, may we be able to ease a little of their pain by showing them how much we care—in our thoughts, in our words, and in what we do. By our actions, may we become closer to You and Your kingdom. Amen."*

Miracle baby

by Paula Kortkamp Harvie

In our files sat the medical reports stating that I would never be able to have a child. Yet against all odds, God had answered our prayers. A little one was on the way. We were ecstatic!

Then six months into this miracle pregnancy, I was diagnosed with breast cancer and was immediately scheduled for a radical mastectomy.

At the time we were living in Guadalajara, Mexico, far from our families. As news of the diagnosis spread among the Christian community, the family of God in Mexico comforted us. These precious brothers and sisters in Christ streamed by our apartment to hug us, weep with us, and pray for us. Never had I experienced such an outpouring of love.

After the last visitor left, Fred and I tried to sleep, but no sleep came. We had too many questions. Would our miracle baby survive? Would its mother live? Fear held our hearts in a vise-like grip. As the dark hours slowly passed, Fred and I reminded each other of favorite Bible verses. We prayed and cried.

Miracle baby

Then in the wee hours of the morning I opened the songbook to a hymn whose words seemed to have been written just for us in this crisis:

"How firm a foundation, ye saints of the Lord,
Is laid for your faith in His excellent Word!
What more can He say than to you He hath said,
To you who for refuge to Jesus have fled?

Fear not, I am with thee, O be not dismayed,
For I am thy God and will still give thee aid;
I'll strengthen thee, help thee,
    and cause thee to stand
Upheld by My righteous, omnipotent hand.

When through fiery trials thy pathway shall lie,
My grace all sufficient shall be thy supply;
The flame shall not hurt thee, I only design
Thy dross to consume and thy gold to refine.

The soul that on Jesus hath leaned for repose,
I will not, I will not desert to his foes;
That soul, though all hell should endeavor to shake,
I'll never, no never, no never forsake!"

The Lord used these words to steady us through my surgery and recovery. Two months later a precious, healthy baby boy arrived. We named him Jonathan, which means "Jehovah has given." God gave him to us when we could not have children. And He gave him to us again by miraculously sparing his life through my cancer surgery.

Worth repeating: This hymn, "How Firm a Foundation," appears to have been first published in 1787 and can be found in many hymnals. It is based on a Bible passage, Isaiah 43:1–2.

Today's prayer: *"Dear God, thank You for being with us in fiery trials and for never forsaking us. Thank You for using hard times to draw us closer to You, to strengthen our faith, and to refine our character. We praise You for Your faithfulness to us in good times and bad. Amen."*

📖 The story behind this story:

The fall of 1997, Paula attended a week-long writers' conference, taking with her a stack of Bible studies she had written and hoped to publish. "What a shame you spent so much time on these," one of the conference directors said, paging through her work. "Nobody is publishing Bible studies."

Paula Harvie came home to El Paso from the conference feeling like she would never be able to fulfill her dream of publishing her ideas and experiences. She was so discouraged that she almost turned down her friend's invitation to come to an introductory "Year of the Family" writing workshop, scheduled two days after her return from the conference. Fortunately for the city of El Paso, Paula attended the workshop and laid aside her discouragement enough to try writing one story ("The mysterious patient," page 69).

"I was amazed that you accepted it and showed me how to re-do it so it could be used. I was grateful to have even one story published," Paula recalled at the end of the project. She went on to become our most prolific previously unpublished writer, publishing 45 columns during the year and, in addition, writing dozens of "wrap-ups" (the sections after each story that include a pertinent Bible quotation and model prayer) for which she received no byline credit.

"'Year of the Family' has been an exciting and unforgettable adventure, totally unforeseen and unexpected," Paula said. - ed.

The family I needed

by Noel Hart

When I was 5 years old my mother could no longer take care of me. So she placed me in the House of Cornelius, a Christian home for children in Fabens, Texas near El Paso. I never knew my dad, but during the 11 years I lived at the home, I was able to see the rest of my family now and then.

I was raised in a good environment at the home but when I reached high school, I became rebellious and started getting into trouble. I did not care about anything and had a lot of anger inside.

People at the House of Cornelius had taught me about the Lord, and I had accepted Him into my heart. But I never really had a good relationship with Jesus. I depended on myself and had trouble allowing others to help me.

The summer after my freshman year I was asked to spend a month with the Harts, a family I knew from Colorado. That way I could get away from everything that was making me stumble. The Harts were missionaries who often came to the House of Cornelius. I had known them since I was 12, and we were good friends. So I went to Colorado to stay with them.

Things then started to change for me. I had a wish that someday I would be able to have a family that would raise me up to be a fine young man. That wish came true, and the Harts legally adopted me March 13, 1997, on my new mom's birthday.

It wasn't easy at first. I went to Faith Christian Academy in Colorado, and I hated it at first. Eventually, though, I grew to love it. During my junior year, I managed to get into some serious trouble that nearly got me kicked out of school. That helped me see the light. I had to make a decision to follow Jesus.

I am living proof that you cannot live your life without trusting God and relying on Him in all situations. I am extremely grateful for what God has done.

If it were not for giving people, I would not be here today. Georgia and Buddy Baca gave of themselves and to the Lord by starting a children's home. If it were not for them, I might not know Jesus. If it were not for my parents, the Harts, giving their lives to the Lord through missions, I probably would not have ever met them, let alone become part of their family. If it weren't for the teachers at Faith Christian Academy giving their time and lives, I would not have the education that I have now. All these people gave to me, but more importantly they gave to God.

I now believe that *"...to whom much is given, from him much will be required* (Luke 12:48b NKJ). God has given me so much, that in return, I need to give back to God and use everything that I have been taught as I go out into the world.

Today's prayer: *"Lord, help me to give back in gratitude for all you and others have given me. Amen."*

 The story behind this story:

This story is part of a speech that Noel Hart gave at his 1998 high school graduation. - ed.

Turning 50

by Jennifer Cummings

A few summers ago I had my 50th birthday. I was taking it pretty well—no serious depression—until I went home to Minnesota to visit family.

I had two aunts in their upper 80s who were living in nursing homes. When I visited Alice, she looked intently at me and said in a surprised voice, "Jennifer, you ARE getting GRAY!"

I said, "Well, yes, but I still feel young," and managed to put the thought aside and go on with our visit.

The next day I visited my other aunt. Bernice said, "Jennifer, you look so young and healthy! How do you do it? You really do have a youthful glow!"

I thanked Bernice for the compliment. Then I couldn't resist telling her about my visit with Alice and that she was surprised at how gray my hair had become.

Vanity about a youthful appearance quickly changed to humility when Bernice said, "Yes, Alice was blessed with better eyesight than I."

Food for thought: We often worry about our appearance...is it imperfect in some way?...a few extra pounds, uninteresting shape, dull hair color, lips too thin, pale skin, freckles, and on and on. We spend money and time trying to change the bodies that God has given us. What are some better ways to spend this money and time?

Worth repeating: The Bible says, *"Charm is deceptive, and beauty is fleeting; but a woman who fears the Lord is to be praised"* (Prov. 31:30).

Today's prayer: *"Dear God, help me to remember that all that I am is a gift from you. Give me a humble attitude and good eyesight, like Alice's, so that my self-vision is clear. Amen."*

Praying for rain

by Annette Horton Herrington

Jay Cantrell unfastened the saddle and slid it off his mare. He arranged his saddle blanket and saddle underneath a white frame church house, set high on fieldstones. Then he slipped a black book from his saddle bag and headed for the front door of the church.

Untrained voices in rough country accents "heisted" a song as he removed his wide-brimmed black hat and stepped inside. The heat was heavy with the warmth of many bodies, in spite of the open windows. As the pump organ wheezed its final note, he strode down the single center aisle past pews of families to sit in front.

When he had been introduced, he stretched out his long frame to stand and, with two steps, he was at the pulpit. Opening the worn pages of the book, he read in a loud voice edged with a twang, *"Ask, and it shall be given you; seek and ye shall find; knock, and it shall be opened unto you: For everyone that asketh receiveth; and* he that seeketh findeth; and to him that knocketh it shall be opened" (Matt. 7:7–8 KJV).

"Brothers," he said, looking into the faces he knew so well, "we are gathered here tonight to pray for rain. We know that without it the crops will wither and many farm families will suffer this year. We also know that God wants what is good for his children and will provide, if we only ask him, believing. I, for one, plan to stay here this evening and pray until the heavens open. I invite all that are able to do the same."

With that statement, he came down from the platform and knelt on the steps, which doubled as an altar. There he began his prayer vigil, sometimes praying audibly, and sometimes with only his lips moving. First one, then another from the farm families came to kneel at his side as he continued to pray.

Minutes, then hours passed. Slowly, some of the folks began to slip out carrying their little ones, limp with sleep, in their arms to the wagons. Some heisted them on their shoulders for the four to five mile walk home. It was black as pitch outside. Still, Jay continued to pray. Others left, but still he prayed.

Finally only a few valiant souls were left to feel the breeze. It started gently but soon rattled the leaves of the nearby woods. It grew in strength until it whistled through the cracks of the church building. Someone secured the horses and boarded up the windows just as the drops started. Soon a rainstorm pounded the parched earth. It was a downpour, a gully-washer—the biggest rain all year! The creeks flooded their banks. The rain continued the next day, gentler now, but steady. Those crops that were not flooded survived.

The story circulated. Brother Jay Cantrell had prayed for rain, and it had come a flood.

"Brother Jay," said his neighbor, "next time, would you mind just praying for dew?"

Food for thought: This story is true. Joshua ("Jay") Cantrell, my great-great grandfather, was a farmer and circuit riding preacher in Cherokee County, Georgia, from (at least) 1868 until he died October 27, 1901. Through succeeding generations, Jay's descendants have revered his legacy of faith and trust in the living God and attempted to pass it on to their children. I am thankful for this dramatic example of how prayer can impact every aspect of our lives.

Today's prayer: *"Thank You, Lord, for those who prayed for me and passed to me a legacy of faith. Help me to pass along a heritage of faith in my turn. Amen."*

Rescuing Joash

by Laura Jane Cerling

In the early 1950s a huge box of second hand-clothing and toys arrived at the Open Door Children's Home in Hazard, Kentucky. Thelma Brown opened it and was sorting the contents when she pulled out the ugliest doll she had ever seen. The body was fixable, but the face was cracked and misshapen.

Who would bother to even pay postage to send such a thing, she thought with disgust. It was always disappointing to her when donors appeared to be thoughtless in the things they sent—as if any old rag or object was good enough for an orphan.

With a sigh, she tossed the doll onto a pile of trash.

Shortly afterwards, Thelma's 4-year-old son, Maurice, came along, looked carefully at the discarded doll, picked it out of the trash, and hugged it. "Mama, I want this doll," he told her.

She started to protest, but he said, "It's so ugly, nobody's ever going to want to love it. And this doll needs to be loved. I'll love her."

Then he named the doll Joash.

In Sunday School the week before, Maurice had heard the Bible story about the wicked woman who killed all her grandchildren so that she could become queen when her son, the king, died. A kind lady rescued Joash, one of the royal grandsons, before he could be killed. Then she raised him in her own family until the people found out that he was alive and made him king.

Maurice was only four, but he had an adopted brother. He knew that sometimes people adopted someone else into their family, rescuing a child from a bad situation.

So Maurice adopted Joash and gave her the love he figured no one else would give her. Several years later, when his family moved to another state, the doll had to go along—even though its owner was half grown by then and his attention was centered elsewhere. As a teen and later as an adult, Maurice still had a tender heart toward those who were being put down by other people.

You never know what might happen – or what you might learn yourself — when you tell a child a Bible story.

Worth repeating: *"...unless you change and become like little children, you will never enter the kingdom of heaven...."* (Matt. 18:3)

Today's prayer: *"Lord, help me to be as responsive to Your words as Maurice was to the Bible story he heard. Amen."*

Learning at home

by Matthew Powers

It was the last time I would ever bounce around on the green seat of the school bus on my way home from school. "My mom's going to teach me at home!" I told my friend. One of the older kids overheard me. He said my parents were weird.

From my first day of school at home, my educational experience differed from my old school mates in first grade. At home I learned in an informal environment instead of a formal school setting. I sat at the kitchen table instead of a desk. My parents were sneaky and fooled me into learning about math, English and science through fun activities.

As the years passed, I learned addition and subtraction by playing board games (it's amazing what dice can teach) and science, geography, history, and English from the books my parents spent hours reading to me. Instead of long days spent sitting in school, I often played outside or took walks in the desert with my mom, where she taught me about plants and animals.

Learning at home

My parents believed in letting me learn at my own pace, so I worked on several different grade levels at once. When people asked me what grade I was in, I replied "I'm in first, second, third, fourth, and sometimes fifth."

Some kids my own age hated school because they felt forced to keep up with everyone else and were branded "stupid" if they couldn't keep pace. Many people believed my parents should put me back in school because of the difficulty I had with reading. Since people believed that all kids should learn on the same timetable, they thought my parents were doing something wrong.

My parents were influenced by Dr. Raymond and Dorothy Moore, the authors of *Better Late Than Early* and *School Can Wait*. The Moores compiled results from over 7000 early childhood studies and concluded that many children like me who had trouble in traditional school would be better off learning informally until age 8 or 10.

Their advice worked for my parents and me. At the age of 10, something clicked inside my brain. All the funny little black scratches inside books took shape and meaning. One week I didn't know the difference between "Frog" and "Fred," and the next I was reading whole books!

I quickly caught up with my friends in reading and was tested at a college reading level three years later. To this day I love to read, but some of my friends burned out through their unfortunate experiences in school and now hate reading.

I am sure I would have been branded "stupid" if I had stayed in school. I am so glad I had encouraging and resourceful parents who believed in me when others would have given up.

Worth repeating: *"Reckless words pierce like a sword, but the tongue of the wise brings healing"* (Prov. 12:18)

Today's prayer: *"Thank you for parents and teachers who have encouraged me. Please encourage them today, too. Amen."*

The story behind this story:

Stories for the "Year of the Family" column came from many places. This story is a short excerpt taken from a paper that Matthew wrote for his freshman English class at the University of Texas at El Paso. A second excerpt from the same paper produced a second column as well, which may be published in a later collection. The story of Matthew's experience as a late-blooming reader has encouraged many local home school parents, giving them hope for their own late-blooming children. Matthew is now an honor student in college.
- ed.

Aunt Virginia

by Jennifer Cummings

"Call me Aunt Virginia and remember, this house is your home while you are in El Paso," Virginia Thomas told young PFC Richard Cummings, a shirt-tail relative stationed at Fort Bliss, nearly a thousand miles from his Oklahoma family.

Virginia Thomas, Native American, born and college educated in Oklahoma, became a dynamic language and drama teacher at El Paso's Bowie High School during the 1950s, 1960s, and early 1970s. She devoted her life to Bowie students until she retired in 1973. She then returned to Oklahoma where she rewrote the Creek Nation constitution before her death in 1986.

"Virginia was a special person," Nolan Richardson, University of Arkansas coach, remembered. "She had that special balance ... sweet and kind, but disciplined and tough. She was totally respected."

"I played football, basketball, baseball," Richardson said, "but Ms. Thomas looked out for the total best interest of her students. She recognized my shyness and helped me learn public speaking, assigning me to give announcements on the PA system and enrolling me in drama clubs."

"We were poor when I was in high school and couldn't afford a Bowie 'Aztec' yearbook," he recalled, "but Ms. Thomas bought one for me. After I went to college, she called now and then to check on me. Later on, when I was coach in Tulsa, Ms. Thomas came to the games ... she was my main girl, sitting right behind the bench!"

Sal Gomez, also a Bowie graduate and student of Ms. Thomas, completed a Navy career and then turned his acting hobby into a second career, appearing in "Walker Texas Ranger," "Unsolved Mysteries," "Lolita," and others. Gomez credits Ms. Thomas with giving him tools for acting.

"Ms. Thomas believed in me," Gomez said. "She encouraged me: 'Don't be intimidated, follow your instincts, go ahead, give it your best!' She inspired me to have confidence in myself."

"Ms. Thomas sponsored the Mask & Gavel Club for the best speakers in Bowie High School," Gomez said. "She coached us for contests in cities throughout the Southwest. That's where I got my roots in public speaking."

The young PFC Cummings that Ms. Thomas took under her wing in the late 1950s has now retired from a successful 24-year military career. "Aunt Virginia coached me on social skills," Cummings said. "I worried about meeting people and what to say, but she said, 'Don't you worry, I'll help you know exactly what to say.' And she did. She introduced me to a general at Fort Bliss. I was nervous, a GENERAL! But Aunt Virginia's coaching saved the day, and our conversation closed with the general saying, 'Welcome Cummings, it's good to have another Okie on post!'"

Virginia Thomas—teacher, aunt, coach, friend—she is no longer living, but the fruit of her teaching is still very much alive in these three men!

Worth repeating: *"The teaching of a wise person gives life. It is like a fountain that can save people from death."* (Prov. 13:14 NCV).

Today's prayer: *"Dear God, thank You for wise teachers like Ms. Thomas, who are sweet and kind, but disciplined and tough. Amen."*

Susan's monkey

by Peter Bulthuis

Growing up as a missionary kid in Africa has benefits and disadvantages. One of the benefits for our 8-year-old daughter, Susan, was having Jackie for a pet.

Jackie was a small gray monkey with a cute black and white face. Susan had him from when he was a couple of months old. She fed him milk from her doll bottle, and her doll buggy was Jackie's bed. He would stay put in the doll buggy when told, except when he saw a dog approaching. Then he would jump up to Susan's shoulder and hide his head in her hair and screech.

I felt apprehensive the first few times Jackie joined the family on hikes up the nearby mountain. I wondered what would happen if Jackie heard all his cousins chattering in the overhead trees. If he would suddenly join them and not return when called, Susan would be heartbroken. But after a few hikes and several scoldings at his wild cousins from the safety of Susan's shoulder, we decided that Jackie thought he was part of this human family and didn't know he was a monkey.

He endeared himself to the family in a special way one Sunday afternoon as the family took a hike at the end of the dry season. Six-foot-high grass on either side of the path cut off the view for the first third of the hike. Jackie, who usually ran behind Susan, suddenly dashed in front of her and tried to trip her. I could not figure out what was happening. When Susan persisted on running up the path, she suddenly screamed, "Jackie bit me on the leg!"

I ran ahead intending to slap Jackie when I looked ten feet ahead of us. In the middle of the path was a six-foot-long spitting cobra, coiled and flipping his head, ready to spit his poisonous venom to blind his victim before striking.

All of the family made a hasty retreat down the path with Jackie bringing up the rear. He was looking back, screeching and scolding the dangerous enemy.

That night when Susan said her evening prayers, she added, "And thank you God for giving monkeys such good eyes that they can see danger that people can't."

Twenty years later when I told this story to Susan's children, 6-year-old Aaron and 3-year-old Sarah, Sarah said, "Papa, I am sure glad Jackie saved my mother's life or she wouldn't even be here with us now, would she?"

Smug Aaron looked at me knowingly and said, "Sarah, if that snake had bitten our mother, you and I wouldn't be here with Papa either!"

Worth repeating: *"In the day of trouble He will keep me safe"* (Psalm 27:5).

Today's prayer: *"Thank You, God, for the protection You give me and my family even when we don't know we are in danger. Amen."*

📖 The story behind this story:

Peter Bulthuis originally published this story in a book he wrote for his children, *Ka Mo Ter Wou*, which means "It is me, your father" in the language of the Tiv tribes-people of Nigeria. To order a copy, write to Peter Bulthuis at 1710 Liberty St., Apt. 103, Lynden, WA 98264. - ed.

The mysterious patient

by Paula Kortkamp Harvie

The patient in Room 116 was a handsome, rich young Mexican architect who kept ending up in the hospital because he was depressed, and he drank too much. The architect came from a prominent family in Guadalajara. He had a big house, fancy cars, and a great future. Yet, he was very unhappy. Something from his past seemed to trouble him.

I noticed that Mrs. G, our nursing supervisor, showed special interest in this patient. Going far beyond her normal duties, she personally gave him his medications, carried his food trays to his room, and cheerfully answered his call bell herself.

And he made lots of calls. He was a grouchy, demanding patient.

"Why is Mrs. G taking care of the patient in 116 herself?" I asked another nurse. "Is she a friend of his or a friend of his family?"

The nurse laughed. "Well, the patient certainly wouldn't think of her as a friend," she said. "Mrs. G knows who the patient is, but he has no idea who *she* is. In fact, he and his family might be pretty upset if they knew who was taking in his food trays and giving him his medications."

"Why is that?" I asked.

"Because a few years ago," the nurse explained, "that patient killed Mrs. G's young nephew."

"What?" I asked. "How?"

"This patient was the leader of a college group playing tricks on new students," she said. "The older boys were drinking too much, things got out of control, and somehow they drowned Mrs. G's brilliant 18-year-old nephew in a campus fountain."

"That's terrible!" I said. "Why isn't this patient in prison?"

"Well, the victim's family did not have the money or political connections to take the older students to court," she explained. "And the students were from well-to-do families. They used their wealth and influence to protect their sons from legal action."

"Mrs. G's sister suffered a nervous breakdown from the terrible grief of losing her only son," she went on. "It has been a very painful experience for the family."

"Then I wonder why Mrs. G is showing him such kindness," I said. "Now, he is at her mercy. She can get back at him. What if she told him who she is? Or, what if she makes a 'mistake' with his medications? Who would know?"

I watched Mrs. G carefully after that. How could she be so cheerful in meeting the architect's constant demands for attention?

In time I learned that Mrs. G had decided long before to leave her nephew's tragic death in the hands of God. She chose to repay evil with goodness. In her view, nursing this patient with kindness was a God-given opportunity to show her forgiveness directly to the one who had caused her family such pain.

The mysterious patient

I don't know what ever happened to the guilty architect. I've heard stories of people like him who have eventually come to peace with God and then turned around and helped others who were hurting. I don't know whether or not he ever did. As with everyone, it was his choice what he did with God's gifts and opportunities, and he may have chosen to reject them.

I do know what Mrs. G's life was like. She had peace and joy; the architect had neither. Mrs.G could have been eaten up with bitterness. Instead, she was happy. She had chosen to deal with her hurt the better way—God's way.

Worth repeating: The Bible says, *"Dear friends, never avenge yourselves. Leave that to God... Instead, do what the Scriptures say: 'If your enemies are hungry, feed them. If they are thirsty, give them something to drink, and they will be ashamed of what they have done to you.' Don't let evil get the best of you, but conquer evil by doing good"* (Romans 12:19–21 NLT).

Food for thought: We all have a choice of how we react when others hurt us. We can hold on to our bitterness and be miserable or, like Mrs. G, we can forgive, let go of our pain and look for ways to show kindness to those responsible for our hurt.

Today's prayer: *""Dear Lord, You know the people who have hurt me and my family. Please show me the better way of dealing with my hurt. Help me to let go of bitterness and trying to get back at others. Instead, help me to show them kindness so that I can enjoy Your peace in my heart. Amen."*

Catching alcoholism

by Bill Schlondrop

When did I catch the disease of alcoholism? I'll tell the story, and you help to decide.

I was born 67 years ago. One of my parents was an alcoholic. Did I become alcoholic in the womb before I was born? Did I catch the disease of alcoholism at the time of my birth?

When I was teething, my parents rubbed whisky on my gums to make the pain go away. Is this when I caught the disease?

In high school I had such a high tolerance for holding alcohol that I became a designated driver, even though the term had not been invented yet. After high school, I joined the Marines. The parties continued throughout the remainder of my 24-year career.

I raised several children and am a grandparent several times over. I got drunk the day my first child was born, when she married, and again at the birth of her first child. Wasn't this an acceptable thing to do?

During several careers, I did many impressive, good things, drinking heavily all the time. Some innovations I created back then are still used today.

Suddenly, my body began giving up the fight. I had to quit drinking. When I made this decision, is this when I became an alcoholic?

I've been involved in a strong recovery program for over six years. I've had the benefit of healing, evolving again, from the egg that grew so long ago. I was sick and I managed to get better. I know the exhilarating feeling of being reborn. I freely admit being an alcoholic, now, after six years of sobriety, finally, I admit feeling normal again.

But what is normal? Is being normal first failing, then admitting and accepting it, and finally turning myself around trying to fix things? If that is the case, I am more normal now, as an admitted alcoholic, free from the booze, than I ever was previously.

If you made a choice, could you say that stress from peer pressure, the environment, or plain alcohol abuse might have contributed to the cause?

The irony of the disease of alcoholism is that after six years of sobriety, I still have the disease whether I drink or not. It isn't important for me to know the exact moment I became an alcoholic, the important thing is that I did something about it. There is a difference between the type of alcoholic I was years ago and the type I am now.

Food for thought: Until we are willing to face our weaknesses and call them by their rightful name, we can't receive help for them. What faults are in your life? First, are you willing to admit them to yourself? Second, will you admit them to a trusted friend who can pray with you?

Worth repeating: The Bible says, *"Confess to one another your faults – your slips, your false steps, your offenses, your sins; and pray for one another that you may be healed and restored"* (James 5:16 AMP).

Today's prayer: *"Dear Lord, I see my areas of weakness and confess them by name to You right now. Help me to overcome these faults that have caused so much hurt to me and to those I love. Please make me whole. Amen."*

Recovery from abortion

by Rosie Chavarría Jones
as told to Becky Cerling Powers

I never in my life thought I would be promiscuous.

I was brought up in a respected, religious El Paso family. I took care of my younger brother and sisters, and they looked up to me as the oldest. After I graduated from high school in 1968, I lived at home, attended UTEP, and worked to pay my college tuition. I had a boyfriend from high school days whom I loved very much. My dream was to marry him as a virgin.

Then he had sex with another girl. It blew my dreams to pieces and my self-respect to pieces, too. In my bitterness I decided to hurt him back. So I went out with different men, and I went to bed with some of them.

When I became pregnant, I was embarrassed. At the time I was working as spokesman for our mayor's Youth Services Bureau. In addition to my university studies, I traveled around the country giving seminars. So I was worried about my image.

I went to the young man I had conceived this child with, but he said he didn't know if he wanted to get married. His family was well known. I was ashamed to have people find out I had conceived out of wedlock. So we decided on an abortion.

But I couldn't live with myself after the abortion. I felt something had been taken away from me. I felt I'd been stripped. I felt it physically, emotionally, and spiritually. I knew I had killed a baby, not a fetus. I looked for someone to talk to, but I felt nobody could understand how I felt.

My high school boy friend wanted to make things right with me again, but I felt too guilty and ashamed to resume the relationship. I didn't want to be close to my family anymore either. I was afraid to be with them, because I might tell what happened and say how I really felt. I wanted to keep up my image, but I knew I was nothing but a fake. I felt ugly, dirty, unworthy...and so alone.

Since I was a little girl I had dreamed of being a wife and mother one day. And then to abort a baby...it was not me. I couldn't live with what I had done. I lost my goals, and I lost meaning for living. I buried my feelings and started to run. I began going out more, and I got myself three jobs – three part-time jobs, plus part-time school and going out, all to keep myself from taking time to sit alone and think.

There were other men, and I became pregnant two more times. I had three abortions in 14 months. After the third one, I started into drugs because I thought it was the way out of everything.

With only 12 hours needed to complete my university degree, I dropped out of school, quit my job with the mayor, and moved to Austin, Texas, so I could get lost in the hippie kingdom of the 1970s. For three years I partied with my hippie friends and used drugs.

Eventually, though, I became tired of not being me, of not being real with myself. I started writing letters to God. I couldn't go to Him one to one, only in letters. I had no basis for knowing I could just go to the Lord and be forgiven. In my letters to God I began to reveal how I really felt. That made me begin to touch base with myself and with Him. I began to hope that I could confess and get the forgiveness I ached for. I realized I wanted to get out of the grave I'd buried myself in with drugs and lies, so I started admitting to people what I'd done.

In the hippie group, people didn't act shocked, so gradually I began to confess the lies I'd been living. When I first admitted with my mouth what I'd done, I felt a little load drop off me. Each time I confessed, a little more load dropped off. Confessing made me feel a little more real as a person. Finally I decided that when I went home for Thanksgiving, I would tell my parents about the abortions.

When I told my mother everything, she cried and cried. Through her tears she said, "I wish you had come to me from the beginning. I don't know what I could have done, but I could have done something. We could have done it together."

Receiving my parents' forgiveness was a big step for me. It caused me to turn around. It made me feel like maybe I could work up to the life I'd wanted since I was a young girl after all, that maybe I could still be fulfilled as a wife and mother and have a nice home. I felt like maybe I could look to that old dream again somehow. I realized I had unfinished business with God, but somehow going to my parents sparked hope. *If they can forgive me*, I thought, *somehow maybe God can forgive me, too.*

I continued to smoke pot and live the hippie life. About a year later I went to a wedding with my cousin. He was snorting cocaine. On the way to a party after the reception, my cousin started driving 90 miles per hour on a dark, narrow, winding country road. He lost control of the car, and we turned over four or five times. I was taking blows to my head, and I lost consciousness. Suddenly I was being sucked into a dark, deep tunnel, and I knew I was heading into hell. I cried out, "My Lord!"

Then I was bathed with a beautiful blue, cool light which turned from a soft blue into white, and I felt a peace upon me. The next thing I knew, I was conscious again and lying in a pool of blood.

Even though the car was in danger of exploding, a girl driving in the car behind us ran over and pulled me out. I had a concussion and traumatized kidneys, and required 18 stitches in my face and hand. I had so many nightmares that the doctor told me I was in shock. He said I had to rest for one month.

So I quit my job and drove to Waco to see Randy and Susie, friends of mine who had become Jesus freaks. I didn't know it, but they had been praying for me. When I arrived they said, "We're going to a Bible study. Do you want to go?"

"I need something," I said. "Take me."

That night God's plan of salvation was laid out before me. I thought, *I've hit a brick wall so hard. What do I have to lose? And I have everything to gain.*

So I confessed, I repented, and I asked Jesus to come into my life. I felt a beautiful warmth come over me like a blanket, like He was saying, "I'm taking care of you from now on." I knew then I'd been cleansed, especially of aborting the babies.

That was January 9, 1976, over 20 years ago. Since then God has blessed me with a Christian husband, a nice home, and a house full of children.

Food for thought: I felt so lonely, reaching out here and there, working, and running to keep myself from my thoughts. Yet, nothing satisfied me because I wasn't being truthful with myself and those I loved. I knew I'd done wrong, but I didn't want to admit it. So I lost identity with Rosie, with the real me.

Today, though, I am like the woman who washed Jesus' feet with her hair. I love him so much because he has forgiven me so much. I am telling my story because more women need to know what he will forgive.

Worth repeating: Jesus said, *"Come to me, all you who are weary and burdened, and I will give you rest. Take my yoke upon you and learn from me, for I am gentle and humble in heart, and you will find rest for your souls. For my yoke is easy and my burden is light"* (Matt. 11:28–30).

Today's prayer: *"Lord God, draw me to Yourself, the source of peace and real joy. Thank You that when You forgive me, I don't have to dwell on the past but can allow You to make me a new creation with a new life. Amen."*

 The story behind this story:

Rosie first told me this story about 10 years ago when the *El Paso Times* asked El Paso women to send their personal abortion stories to the "Living" department for a special feature. Rosie had no time to write her story, so I took notes and wrote it as an "as told to" account. Later the "Living" editor decided to drop the abortion project.

So Rosie's story remained unpublished until "Year of the Family," when I dug it out, reworked it, and, with Rosie's blessing, published it as a continuing story in three columns. By 1998 Rosie had eight children and was busy home schooling them with her husband. We'd both had more time to write and correct the story 10 years ago than we had when I really needed it. - ed.

Grandma thinks fast

by Jennifer Cummings

Grandma always wore an apron, full length, with a bib to protect her blouse and a gathered bottom to cover her skirt. But could this apron provide protection from what Grandma would face later that afternoon?

Grandma lived with our family in rural Minnesota in the 1950s. One summer Sunday afternoon we visited Uncle Jack. His farm had wooded areas and pastures in which berries grew wild. Grandma, pail in hand, announced that she was going to pick berries in the pasture.

"Look out for the sheep buck," Uncle Jack said. "He likes to terrorize berry pickers."

Undaunted, Grandma headed into the pasture. Soon, in her peripheral vision, she spotted the sheep buck heading her way. He gained speed and came faster, faster!

Grandma calmly walked to a nearby tree stump and covered it with her apron skirt. Then she stood firmly behind the stump, and the sheep buck rammed his target—Grandma's apron covering the stump.

That sheep never bothered Grandma again.

Food for thought: Grandma's apron protected against food stains but gave no protection against the charging sheep. Yet she was not afraid. God had promised to be with her. She used the gifts God had given her—creativity, an apron, and the nearby tree stump—to keep her safe from danger.

Worth repeating: *"For the LORD gives wisdom, and from his mouth come knowledge and understanding. He holds victory in store for the upright, he is a shield to those whose walk is blameless, and he guards the course of the just and protects the way of his faithful ones"* (Prov. 2:6–8 NIV).

Today's prayer: *"Dear God, thank You for your promise to be with me and give me wisdom through all of the dangerous and difficult times of my life. Help me to remember and trust in that promise. At the same time, help me recognize and work with what You give me, the way Grandma did. Amen."*

Dreaming of Anita Jo

by Paula Kortkamp Harvie

We were just 19 and had all of life ahead of us—or so we thought. After my good friend Anita Jo and I finished our sophomore year at Baylor University, she went off to church camp, and I went to Dallas for summer school.

One muggy July afternoon the phone rang. "Anita Jo was in a car accident in West Texas," a solemn voice said. "She was killed instantly."

The news plunged me into a whirlpool of grief. I had lost three grandparents by then, but this was different. Death had cruelly snatched away a young person with great promise, someone my own age. How could I cope?

A deep sadness engulfed me that summer. I was a student nurse rotating through pediatrics at Baylor Hospital. Many of our precious little patients were dying from leukemia, which in the 1950s was incurable. Death was all around me.

In an odd way, I felt guilty for living. Anita Jo was a gifted pianist and vocalist. She was popular on campus and active in many organizations. She had so much to offer the world. I, on the other hand, mistakenly felt I was nobody and had no particular talent. Surely the Lord had made a terrible mistake. He should have spared Anita Jo and taken me instead.

Often I dreamed about my friend being in a terrible car wreck, but she always survived. Sometimes in my dreams she even got up out of her casket.

Finally, I dreamed about my friend one last time. As always, the dream began with Anita Jo being critically injured in an accident but living through it. This time, however, the dream ended differently. After surviving the accident, Anita Jo was diagnosed with leukemia and faced prolonged suffering and certain death. I woke up, sobbing. "Lord," I cried, "it would have been much better for You to have taken her instantly in the car accident rather than let her suffer and die from leukemia!"

After that final dream, I never again questioned God about Anita's Jo's death. Instead I thanked Him that she had not suffered and was now in heaven, using her beautiful voice to sing in the celestial choir.

Food for thought: After the accident, the driver of the car in which Anita Jo was killed found her New Testament lying open on the pavement. When he picked it up, he saw these words she had underlined: *"For to me to live is Christ, and to die is gain"* (Phil. 1:21 KJV). Because Anita Jo had a personal relationship with Jesus Christ, she did not fear death. She saw death as merely the doorway to a far better life with her Lord.

Today's prayer: *"Father, there are things in life we'll never understand, but we trust You anyway. We know You never make mistakes. Your ways are far superior to ours. Thank You for the hope of eternal life through Your Son, Jesus Christ. And thank You for the joy we'll experience some day when we're reunited with our loved ones in heaven. Amen."*

📖 The story behind this story:

The same day that this story was published in the features section of the *El Paso Times*, headlines in the "Borderland" section proclaimed the tragic news that a mother and her 9- and 12-year-old daughters had been crushed to death between two semi-trucks in a construction-related accident on the interstate. Their deaths seemed needless and incomprehensible—just like Anita Jo's death.

Stunned by the coincidence of the two stories being published on the same day, Paula prayed that her story might help to comfort people who would be struggling with the same "Why?" question that her dream addressed 40 years before. A few days later, while attending a support group for relatives of Alzheimer's victims, she learned one answer to her prayer. When group members started talking about how much they appreciated the daily "Year of the Family" stories, one woman brought up the story of Anita Jo. She said her 12-year-old granddaughter had been best friends with the 12-year-old girl who died in the car accident. So she had cut out and given the column to her granddaughter to comfort her. Another part of this story behind the story is told next. - ed.

Early lessons pay off

by Francis A. Diaz

    The last Sunday my family had together alive was six weeks ago, August 2, 1998. We attended evening service at Harvest Christian Center like we always did, and at the end of the service I felt led by the Lord to go up to the front with them to pray. My wife, Janine, stood behind us while I knelt with our two daughters, 12-year-old Lydia and 9-year-old Ana.
    I put my hands on their heads and said, "God, I'm here to tell you that I know these children are Yours. I know that YOU know that, but I want You to know that I know it, too. Your will be done."
    Janine and I were very concerned with how Lydia and Ana were growing up, but we made sure that before they received intellectual, physical, or social training, they received spiritual training. We started as soon as they were born. From before the time they could say "Mommy" or "Daddy," we prayed for them, sang to them, and read to them from the Bible about God and the good news of Jesus Christ.

Eventually our daughters learned to speak, read, write, do arithmetic, play games, and make friends. But their Bible training came first and foremost. We started that soon because we were never sure how long we would be with them to do this for them. We wanted them to get to heaven when they were old.

How old? As old as they ever got to be.

"You've got ministries today," I used to tell them. "You can't wait till you grow up or till you marry. Today you have to carry out your ministry."

And they did. I've been sick the past five years from complications after I got hepatitis. My heart stopped, my kidneys and liver kicked out, and my lungs collapsed. I survived partly because they waited on me hand and foot. They did everything for me.

"Blessed am I, among women," I used to joke. They were wonderful girls, absolutely beautiful.

That last Sunday night together, it had just been a few weeks since I'd been feeling well again. The following Tuesday we visited Carlsbad Caverns. It was our first big family outing in five years.

The next day, Wednesday, August 5, 1998, my wife and daughters were coming home from a picnic in Las Cruces when their car was crushed between two semi-trucks in a construction-related highway accident. Suddenly, they were called home to be with their Maker. Lydia and Ana weren't very old, but they were old enough. At that very moment, their training paid off.

I never expected to have to do without my children. I assumed, as every parent does, that they would have to do without me some day. But, you never know. To paraphrase David in 2 Sam. 12:23, *"I can't bring them back, but I will go to them."*

Today, I am lonely. Yet, I am thankful that Janine and I kept God first and started early teaching our daughters to keep Him first, too. They were trained in the right

Early lessons pay off

way to go, and from Heaven they will never depart, regardless of how long eternity rolls.

Family resource: Francis Diaz's church has made available three audio tapes of the Diaz family's story: the memorial service August 11, Francis's story of the family's faith shared with the congregation the evening of August 9, and Pastor Eddy Lee's morning sermon August 9, "Why the Righteous Suffer." Tapes are $2.50 each plus $1 postage (covers 1 to 3 tapes). Contact Harvest Christian Center, 785 Southwestern Drive, El Paso, TX 79912. (915) 585-9934

 The story behind this story:

At the funeral service for Janine, Lydia, and Ana Diaz, Francis told his grieving friends that not long before his wife died, she had told him, "I not only want my life to count for Christ. I want my death to count even more for Christ." One of Francis's listening friends was a writer for "Year of the Family." The friend thought that writing a tribute to his family's faith for "Year of the Family" would help Francis to express his grief and, at the same time, would give him a way to honor his wife's wish. So a few weeks afterward, he suggested the idea to Francis, who then phoned me and sent me this column for editing. - ed.

The church is family

by Néaouguen Nodjimbadem
as told to Becky Cerling Powers

My father was one of the early Christian believers in the African nation of Chad. When we were kids, he took us to church every Sunday. Then every Wednesday and Friday he took us to prayer meetings. The church had a huge parking lot where the kids loved to play soccer. They played there all the time. So while we were sitting next to our father inside the church doing Bible studies and praying, we could hear the other kids playing in the parking lot.

We didn't like it. We didn't have a resentment against church, but we would have liked to be outside playing. We had no choice about it, though. For my dad, it was important to attend prayer meetings to show us what he saw as essential for our lives. He believed that the only way for people to grow spiritually was to be active in Bible study and prayer meetings at church. What was great was that after church, my dad played baseball and soccer with us.

The church is family

Today I am really happy that my father insisted on taking us to church Fridays, Wednesdays, and Sundays—all the time. My parents' insistence that we go to church influenced my life permanently, and it increased my love for the church when I was not with my family.

During civil war in Chad, there were massive killings. In 1982, my dad told me, "You've got to leave Chad. It's people like you they are trying to kill." I was a teacher, and he saw that the government was targeting educated people.

After leaving Chad, I went to a country where Christians could not openly express their faith in Christ. Still, when I met Christians for Bible studies and worship services, I shared with them the heavy burden of my loneliness and my concern for my family living in danger back home. They prayed for my country and my family, and this made me feel good because I was not alone. We supported each other. The owners of the home where we met for church made their home a home for us. It was really a family.

Here in El Paso my church family is so important. My wife and I find friendship and love there. People care for us. It's a family, a real family life for me, being a part of a church, far from my own family in Chad. And this discovery of the family life of the church was made possible because of what my parents taught me as a young kid.

Food for thought: People need to know that the church is supposed to be a place where everybody has his place and everybody feels at home because we are sharing the same faith, the same love of God, and we have the same Christ. Because of that, the church can be a real family.

My Roots Go Back to Loving

Worth repeating: Jesus said those who follow him are his family: *"Whoever does the will of my Father in heaven is my brother and sister and mother"* (Matt. 12:49-50).

Today's prayer: *"Help me, Heavenly Father, to be an obedient child in Your family. Amen."*

📖 The story behind this story:

Today's simmering war in Chad began in the early 1970s, Nodji (Néaouguen Nodjimbadem) says, and it has caused Christians much suffering. During a time of persecution when President Tombalbaye's soldiers were closing down churches and burying pastors alive, Nodji's father and other church leaders courageously opposed the government. They were scheduled for execution on April 13, 1975, but a *coup d'etat* saved their lives.

Chad enjoyed relative peace for four years until civil war broke out again in 1979. Nodji's story about rescuing his extended family from the battlefield is on page 37. Conflict flared up again during the summer of 1982 when Hisseine Habré sent troops to conquer the christianized south. At that point, Nodji's father advised him to flee Chad.

Between 1982 and 1984, Habré's soldiers disrupted Christian worship services by setting churches on fire and shooting everyone who tried to escape the flames. Christians were often targeted by both sides in the war, because they refused to side with either the government or the rebellion. In 1984, Nodji's father was arrested and imprisoned. After his release, he lived under house arrest for two years, then died Dec. 26, 1986. Nodji believes that his father's prison experiences caused his relatively early death at age 62.

When Nodji visited Chad in 1996, he found that the church had strengthened and multiplied during his absence. Every church burned by soldiers had been replaced by three or four new churches. - ed.

Psalm 91: antidote to insomnia

by Paula Kortkamp Harvie

It was the spring semester of my senior year in high school in Oklahoma. My dad was in the Navy and had left for sea duty, shuttling between San Francisco and Japan. Mother had gone back to Illinois to care for my grandfather during the final weeks of his life. Seventeen years old, I was home alone.

Although I would admit it to no one, I was afraid to go to sleep at night. I didn't fully trust my little Chihuahua to keep me safe. Too ashamed to ask my friends to stay with me, I turned to the Lord for protection. Every night I repeated Psalm 91 over and over until I could peacefully fall asleep. Soon I had memorized this wonderful psalm. It has been a favorite ever since.

"Those who live in the shelter of the Most High will find rest in the shadow of the Almighty. This I declare of the LORD: He alone is my refuge, my place of safety; he is my God and I am trusting him. For he will rescue you from every trap and protect you from the fatal plague. He will

shield you with his wings. He will shelter you with his feathers. His faithful promises are your armor and protection. Do not be afraid of the terrors of the night, nor fear the dangers of the day, nor dread the plague that stalks in darkness, nor the disaster that strikes at midday. Though a thousand fall at your side, though ten thousand are dying around you, these evils will not touch you. But you will see it with your eyes; you will see how the wicked are punished."

"If you make the LORD your refuge, if you make the Most High your shelter, no evil will conquer you; no plague will come near your dwelling. For he orders his angels to protect you wherever you go. They will hold you with their hands to keep you from striking your foot on a stone. You will trample down lions and poisonous snakes; you will crush fierce lions and serpents under your feet!"

"The LORD says, 'I will rescue those who love me. I will protect those who trust in my name. When they call on me, I will answer; I will be with them in trouble. I will rescue them and honor them. I will satisfy them with a long life and give them my salvation" (Psalm 91 NLT).

Food for thought: God has promised His children divine protection in dangerous situations if we ask Him. Frightening circumstances can be golden opportunities for God to show us His loving care and powerful protection.

Today's prayer: *"Heavenly Father, thank You for promising to answer me when I call to You to be with me in trouble and rescue me. Help me not to waste time worrying about my protection but to trust You completely with my care. Amen."*

My two dads

by Janimarie Rowe
as told to Becky Cerling Powers

Since I had the same last name as my mom and dad, I was 8 years old before I started to wonder why I was the toddler in my parents' wedding pictures. When I asked Mom about it, she told me that I had two fathers, my biological dad, Sam, and the man I knew as "Dad," my dad Ron, who had adopted me and was raising me.

That was a shock. Memories of my dad Sam began surfacing, and I began having dreams about him every couple months, wondering what he was like. Mom always assured me that he had loved me. She said that I had been the ultimate Daddy's Girl. But he had never contacted me after Mom and Dad married. I wondered why he hadn't even sent me a birthday card. I always assumed that one day I'd meet him and find out.

Today, as an adult, I realize that much of the resentment I felt toward my dad Ron growing up probably had its roots in that severed bond. My dad Sam had spoiled me. When my parents married, I was 22 months old, and my dad Ron adopted me. He wanted to be a good Christian parent, and he was. He saw a little girl who was spoiled, and he wanted to change that now that he was her daddy. That was something I couldn't understand until I was older.

When my sister, Shauna, came along a couple of years later, her personality meshed better with Dad's than mine. I wasn't jealous of Shauna. She and I were good friends. But my dad Ron and I had a lot of conflicts. In high school, it often crossed my mind that he was not my father. I felt like the black sheep in the family.

When I married Steve at age 18, I began praying that God would take away the anger I had toward my dad Ron. A year later, baby Josh was born. About that time, I saw a TV talk show about finding a parent you'd never seen before. When I told my mom about it, she mentioned that Dad had had a dream that my dad Sam had died.

That scared me. I had always assumed my biological dad would show up some day. It had never occurred to me that he might die before I met him. What if he never saw my baby?

I told my parents I wanted to find my dad Sam and they said they'd help me any way they could. They gave me the name of Sam's father, my biological grandfather, who lived in El Paso. My biological dad's father and mother had divorced when Sam was 13 years old.

When I phoned, this grandfather said he hadn't heard from Sam in ten years, and he had no idea where he was. But the next day, on Christmas Eve 1993, he called to say he had found his ex-wife's mother's phone number in South Carolina.

My biological great-grandmother in South Carolina put me in contact with my dad Sam's mother, my biological grandmother. She told me that my dad Sam was in prison in California. She also said that he had been married and divorced three times altogether, so I had six younger brothers and sisters.

I couldn't call my dad Sam in prison, but I wrote, and he wrote back immediately. We bonded right away and started writing to each other three times a week. Almost every day there was a letter coming one way or the other. He said he had become a Christian in prison, and he was now teaching Bible studies there.

I told him all about my life, and he told me all about his. A lot of kids who find their parents are disappointed because their parents turn them away, but he was wonderful. He said he'd been asked by a family member not to contact me until I contacted him. That's why he hadn't tried to get in touch with me all those years. He called me pet names like Angel and said I would now and forever be Daddy's Girl.

We started writing in early January 1994. We wrote for three months, and then he was finally released from prison. He flew to El Paso in early April. I went to the airport with 5-month-old Josh and stood watching and waiting as all these men came off his plane. The only picture I had of him was from back when he was a hippie, so I didn't know what he looked like. I felt like God was telling me to really cherish this moment.

When he got off the plane, we were both crying. He came on a Wednesday and left the next Monday morning. We talked constantly. He kept saying, "Now God can take me because my life is complete. I've seen you and I've seen my grandson."

We agreed that my husband and I would drive to California on Memorial Day weekend to meet the five children from his third marriage. When I took him to the airport Monday morning, I didn't know why I felt so depressed. I thought I'd see him in six weeks.

That next Saturday morning, his mother phoned. My dad Sam had died the night before of an embolism.

My mom was out of town, so I called my sister, Shauna, and she called my dad Ron. He phoned me sobbing. He kept saying, "I'm so sorry." That was when the truth finally dawned: "He really does love me."

For a year I'd been praying that God would take away the anger that I had toward my dad Ron. Somehow, at that moment, it happened. The hurts and pains I had had inside, and my interpretations of the way things had happened with my dad Ron, all just disappeared. When my dad Sam died, all that died with him. I realized God had given my dad Ron and me to each other, and it's been different between us ever since.

I had to take care of most of the funeral arrangements in California because my dad Sam was no longer married to his third wife, and I was the oldest child. It was hard meeting my five little brothers and sisters, ages 3 to 12. They were raised differently from me. They grew up in a home where their mom did drugs and had other men living with her after my dad Sam went to prison.

At the graveside ceremony, with Josh in my arms and the little kids jumping around, I began to feel a sense of *deja vu*. Suddenly, I realized I was reliving a dream I'd had when I was little. In the dream there were rolling green hills in the background just like these. I was holding a baby, and dark-headed kids were jumping around me.

I felt great love from God that day. He spared my dad Sam's life for a few months so that I was able to see him, and He healed my relationship with my dad Ron. I sensed how much my Heavenly Father cared about me and all of us. I saw that God wants families to be restored.

Worth repeating: The Bible says, *"While they are still talking to me about their needs, I will go ahead and answer their prayers"* (Isaiah 65:24b NLT).

Today's prayer: *"Thank You, God, that You know our deepest needs and are able to meet them. Thank You for Your constant care and faithfulness. Amen."*

📖 The story behind this story:

A powerful story carries an extra punch when it involves local people. Readers suddenly realize that they know these folks! Janimarie's parents and grandparents started getting lots of phone calls from old friends after this story was published, and people at her dad's business came in to his office with tears in their eyes after they read it. - ed.

Mom's mouthwash

by Virginia Payne Steely

I remember it like it was yesterday. I was 7 or 8 years old, and I had just uttered "that word."

My mother grabbed me by the shoulder and said, "Young lady, you march yourself into the bathroom right now. You are getting your mouth washed out with soap. We don't use that kind of language in this house."

Washing my mouth out with soap did the trick. I still know what Ivory soap tastes like. "That word" was never used again.

I had heard a playmate use the new word, and being a child, I had to try it on for size. I was grown before I knew what "that word" meant. Mama was right. We didn't use "that word" in our house.

Children like to experience new words and sounds. "Sycamore" was a special word for a neighbor's boy. Matthew liked to say it. The sound pleased him. "I'm going to the sycamore tree, the sycamore tree," he would yell gleefully.

Children like the sounds of rhymes and fairy tales. Children learn from words spoken by family, friends, and TV actors and words read in books. They need to learn which words are proper to use and which should be left unsaid.

In today's world, mouth washing with soap might not be in vogue, but it worked for me.

Food for thought: The following scripture gives a clue to people who want to clean up their language. Paul says that words of thanks and words that build people are up are appropriate, while smutty jokes and foul language are not. He links having a thankful spirit with having a clean life and clean language. Nurturing a thankful attitude cleans up dirty talk better than Ivory soap.

Worth repeating: In the Bible, the apostle Paul said, *"Do not let any unwholesome talk come out of your mouths, but only what is helpful for building others up according to their needs, that it may benefit those who listen.... But among you there must not be even a hint of sexual immorality, or of any kind of impurity, or of greed, because these are improper for God's holy people. Nor should there be obscenity, foolish talk, or coarse joking, which are out of place, but rather thanksgiving"* (Eph. 4:29, 5:3–4 NIV).

Today's prayer: *"Help me, Lord, to recognize my blessings today and take time to thank You. Amen."*

Susie's first funeral

by Jennifer Cummings

Although the innocence of childhood prevented my 5-year-old niece, Susie, from fully understanding death, she was respectful, attentive, and eager to face the mysteries surrounding the death of her grandfather.

When my father died, my two youngest brothers and I had a total of 10 children between the ages of 5 and 10 years old. This was their first encounter with the death of a close relative. I was concerned that they would be frightened when they saw Grandpa's body in the casket, or when they saw dirt being shoveled onto the casket after it was lowered into the grave.

Before the funeral, I gathered the 10 children, including Susie, and talked to them about death. I explained, "When a person dies, the soul—the real person—goes to heaven; the body—just an empty body—stays here on earth, and we put it in the ground. When you see Grandpa's body in the casket, don't be frightened or worry about him because he has already gone to heaven where he is safe and happy."

The funeral day came. We attended the church service and the graveside service. Although the children were sad about their Grandpa's death, no one was surprised or frightened by the day's events.

After the graveside service, the women of the church served a lunch in the church basement. Mrs. Chaffee, who was about 90 years old, helped serve the lunch. Her hair was thin and white, her face was pale and wrinkled from many years of living, her body was stooped with age, but she was still serving others.

When Susie saw Mrs. Chaffee, she went quietly over to her father and said, "Daddy, Daddy, why is her body still here?"

Food for thought: We can laugh at Susie's misunderstanding that Mrs. Chaffee was already dead, that we had just neglected to bury her body. But there was no bad intent, no evil motive. Susie believed what I had told her about death. She did not question me. She did not ask for proof. She simply believed. This willingness to believe is a good example of childlike innocence. What can we do to hold on to our childlike innocence as we grow older?

Worth repeating: *"I tell you the truth, anyone who will not receive the kingdom of God like a little child will never enter it"* (Mark 10:15).

Today's prayer: *"Dear God, at times I struggle with my inability to understand the mysteries of your kingdom. Sometimes I am tempted to say, 'This doesn't make sense. It can't be true.' I ask you to help me to simply believe, just like Susie did. Amen."*

Home schooling chaos

by Becky Cerling Powers

Home schooling our children was such a rewarding experience that by the end of each school year, I was willing to do it another year. The beginning of each school year was a different story, though.

Every year frustration took over as I faced the task of setting up the new school year. I felt overwhelmed, drowning in details—all those books to look through, subjects to plan, music lessons and sports activities to schedule, a house to manage, a home school support group to lead, and on and on.

Then one year, in the middle of the annual mess, I read the first chapter of Genesis in the Bible. As I read, it struck me that Genesis 1 not only says God created the earth, it also describes *the creative process.*

In Genesis 1, God started with a giant massiveness that was *"without form."* It was empty and covered in darkness. That sounded just like what I faced at the beginning of each school year!

Then God spoke out his thoughts and began making separations. He created light, then separated light from darkness. He named things: He *"called the light 'day,' and the darkness he called 'night.'"* The next day God created *"the expanse."* He separated the water under the expanse from the water above it, calling the expanse *"sky."* The next day God made another distinction: *"land"* and *"sea."* And he did something with the land: He caused it to produce vegetation.

So it went. God began with a formless void, then made separations and distinctions. He developed patterns. He established routines. He gave names and meaning to what He had created.

I realized that every process people generally label "creative" involves these same activities. A composer selects certain rhythms and notes from a chaos of notes and rhythms (separating, distinguishing). With these he develops patterns—musical themes, harmony. An artist selects a certain medium and then creates form and pattern where once all was formless and meaningless—just a pile of tools and background materials like paper, tile, or clay

What I was really facing at the beginning of each school year was an opportunity to fulfill my creative nature as someone made in God's image. So, instead of getting frustrated with the formless void, I needed to rejoice. For this was the start of another adventure in creativity. I needed to work with the process and trust the God of the process. Then, as I worked alongside Him, that creative process would produce a kind of new world.

The school year would not remain a formless void. I would be able to make separations, to establish patterns and routines, to bring form to what was formless and meaning to what seemed meaningless. I would be able to turn chaos into order, and even, with God helping me, to cause life and growth within that new order.

So I've learned to start thanking God now whenever that familiar sense of frustration hits. Whatever project I'm working on, that's my clue that I am, once again, facing the adventure of creativity.

Today's scripture: Genesis 1

Today's prayer: *"Lord, help me to trust You in my work today. Amen."*

📖 **The story behind this story:**

Stories for the "Year of the Family" column showed up in odd places. Sometimes when we were short on material, I would suddenly find or remember something usable. This story came from a letter that I had written to our son Erik in graduate school two years before the "Year of the Family" writing project. Erik had written home first, describing his frustration in the lab at Washington State University researching *Rhizobium meliloti.* I knew nothing whatsoever about *R. meliloti.* I couldn't even pronounce it, much less spell it without checking twice. But from Erik's description I recognized the symptoms of somebody struggling with the creative process. Our son was facing a big project that seemed dark and formless, and he was trying to make sense of it by drawing a map. I sent a letter to encourage him and explain how insights from the first chapter of Genesis had once helped me in my own struggles with the creative process. I stumbled across a copy of that letter in my file two years later just when I needed material for the column. It was simple to modify an excerpt from the letter to meet the space requirements for the daily story. - ed.

Glad I listened

by Laura Jane Cerling

"My mom's cancer has flared up again," my son's best friend, Lyle, told me on a visit home from college. "This is the third time. Would you please go visit her?"

As I looked into his troubled eyes, it was easy to say, "Of course."

Keeping the promise was harder. I knew Lyle's mother only by sight. Our families were linked only through the friendship of our sons and the knowledge that we all were Christians. My knees were knocking when I made that first visit to Betty, but her obvious pleasure brought me back often. Before long, we found many common interests.

"My mom really appreciates your visits," Lyle said on his next visit home. "Somehow she's not getting many visits from some of her oldest friends." As I thought about his comment, I wondered if it was just too painful for these people to visit a dying friend.

Betty's illness lasted several years, and during that time she had several rallying periods, followed by decline. My deep concern slacked off with the press of my large family's activities. Then one day as I was loading groceries into my car, the thought came, "You've not seen Betty for a long time."

An unspoken dialogue started. "I've got no time for a visit—not today!"

But the persistent inner voice said, "You really should check and see how she's doing."

I gave in. Soon I was letting myself into the family's back door. "It's Laura Jane!" I called.

Betty was alone. Her face was turned to the wall, and she was crying. I stood before her bed with my hand on her shoulder, wanting so much to comfort, but having no words. Then I heard myself singing, "I will sing of my Redeemer, of His wondrous love to me. On the cruel cross He suffered, paid the debt and set me free."

The words of the hymn seemed to give her strength. She turned over, dried her eyes, and we talked of many things. As always, I prayed with her before I left. Even on hard days there are reasons to praise God, and that day I had special reason to give thanks, because I had listened to that quiet voice insisting I make the visit.

That evening our phone rang. "Thank you for visiting my wife today," Lyle's father said. "It had to be the Lord who sent you. It was such a bad day for Betty. I didn't want to go to work, but I felt I had to leave her those few hours until our daughter would come home."

Food for thought: Generally, God speaks to us through His Word, the Bible. But He is not limited. That day God's hurting child needed a human messenger to bring the reassurance of His love. I'm glad I obeyed.

Worth repeating: Like the little boy, Samuel, in the Bible, we need to say sincerely to God, *"Speak, Lord, for your servant is listening"* (1 Sam. 3:9b).

Today's prayer: *"Help me, O Lord, to practice listening to Your voice and obeying it in little things today, so that I will be prepared to hear and obey if You ever call on me to do big things. Amen."*

 The story behind this story:

At the beginning of the "Year of the Family" project, before we had many writers yet, my mother (Laura Jane Cerling) dug out old copies of her church newsletter in which she had written personal reflections and stories based on interviews with people from the church. It was a treasure store of usable material for the column. This story was part of what she sent. I had always suspected that my mother could write for publication, given the right opportunity. She was unaware of her gift, though. Mom just saw writing as a way to enrich the lives of her family and friends through stimulating letters and stories in her church's newsletter. Through "Year of the Family" my 77-year-old mother found she loved the mental challenge of meeting deadlines and writing to a format. And I loved being able to open a door to publication for her work. For in this way, "Year of the Family" gave me an opportunity to share my mother's wisdom (one of the great treasures of my life) with the city I love. During that year, Mom published 28 columns with a byline and also wrote dozens of column wrap-ups (scriptures and prayers at the ends of stories) for which she received no byline credit. - ed.

Grandma's Christmas in July

by Zula McKenzie

My family is so large that we hold one party a month to celebrate whoever has a birthday or whatever holiday comes that month. It is a perfect chance to get the family together to catch up on all the "goings on."

One November I watched as the calendars came out of the computer. January showed three birthdays. February showed up next with Valentine's Day and another birthday.

Holding up my hand to stop the printing, I told Randi, who was making the calendars, to add July 25th: Grandma's Christmas Party. She looked at me like I had finally flipped my gray wig.

I had decided that instead of giving presents to the great grandchildren at Christmas, I would save them till July. That way they would have new toys in the middle of the year. With parents, grandparents, aunts and uncles, the children get so many gifts, there is utter confusion.

That Christmas, one of the kids asked why I hadn't given any gifts. Then I announced that we would have Grandma's Christmas in July.

When the sales came after Christmas, I was ready in my track shoes, pushing and shoving like a pro. I had shopping bags for each child, and in these I dropped snow globes, dolls for the girls, tops for the boys. The Christmas candy went in the freezer. There were Santa Claus drinking mugs, puzzles, and other toys, all bought on sale. Later I bought water pistols for each child, along with bubble blowers. Just before party time I bought bathing suits for each one.

On the big day, I decorated the table with a white tablecloth and a small Christmas tree. Around the tree I arranged the Santa mugs, filled with lemonade. The temperature was 100° outside, but the air conditioner kept the house cool. Everyone arrived in high spirits. We sang Christmas carols and drank lemonade.

We seated the eight children in a circle, and I brought out shopping bags. Each bag had at least eight gifts. One of the gifts was a personal battery-operated fan, and these were soon twirling away. When all the items had been inspected, I passed around the last gift, the bathing suits. Then the little girls gave us a fashion show in their new suits, but the little boys were too bashful.

After the show, I told the kids to go to the back yard, fill their water guns and have a good time. The adults joined the kids in the yard and enjoyed the water fight, too.

At dusk we brought in the children, dried them off, and served cake and ice cream. The children, now three years older, still talk about Grandma's Christmas in July, a Christmas they won't ever forget.

Worth repeating: The Bible says, *"The wise woman builds her house, but with her own hands the foolish one tears hers down"* (Prov. 14:1).

Today's prayer: *"Dear Heavenly Father, show me creative, loving ways to build up my family. Amen."*

 The story behind this story:

Zula originally wrote this story as part of her activities in the El Paso Writers' League. When writer Mary Ann Herman read it, she said, "You should send that story in to 'Year of the Family.'" Zula did, and here it is. - ed.

Faith vs. fear

by Paula Kortkamp Harvie

Fear is a lousy companion. I know. He lived with me for almost three years. While expecting our son, Jonathan, I was diagnosed with cancer. The physical scars from the resulting surgery were nothing compared to the emotional scars. Fear had forced his way into my soul and taken up residence as an unwelcome guest.

After that, the slightest ache or pain sent me running to the doctor, with Fear taunting me all the way. As soon as the doctor said he found no cancer, Fear slunk away to wait for another day.

One of his favorite tricks was a campaign of whispers, "What if ___?" My overactive imagination filled in the blanks. Every time I played this game with him, his old crony, Depression, bullied his way in. Then hours or days passed in misery. I seemed unable to get rid of my dreadful visitors.

In spite of this ongoing battle with Fear, I longed for another baby. I talked to the Lord about it regularly, always adding, "But Lord, if I'm not going to live, I don't want to bring another child into the world. May Your will be done."

We were thrilled when we learned God was blessing us with a second child. Four months into the pregnancy, I went to Houston for my regular checkup at a cancer hospital. Seeing my maternity clothes, the doctor blurted, "You're pregnant? You, with a history of cancer?" Then the upset doctor discovered a small lump under my arm. "Go on back to El Paso," he said brusquely. "After you deliver in five months, we'll do a biopsy."

I returned home an emotional wreck, with Fear cackling in the shadows. How would I make it through the next five months?

Out of the blue, a high school friend I had not seen in years called me from a distant city. "Paula, what in the world is going on?" she asked. "The Lord woke me up last night to pray for you, and I can't get you off my mind." Amazed, I poured out my story. She prayed with me over the phone and asked God to heal me.

The next morning I sat down on the couch to read my beloved Amplified New Testament. Desperate for comfort, I turned to Philippians, where I came to some favorite verses. In these particular circumstances, they took on a deeper meaning.

"Do not fret or have any anxiety about anything, but in every circumstance and in everything by prayer and petition with thanksgiving continue to make your wants known to God. And God's peace will be yours, that tranquil state of a soul assured of its salvation through Christ, and so fearing nothing from God and content with its earthly lot of whatever sort that is, that peace which transcends all understanding, shall garrison and mount guard over your hearts and minds in Christ Jesus" (Phil. 4:6,7 AMP).

As I read those words, the peace of God mounted guard over my imagination, blocking the taunts of my old enemy. Fear was still yelling "What if?" but now I was safe from his torment, and he left.

Four months later our son David was born, and the lump mysteriously disappeared. God had answered our prayers.

Food for thought: Since that experience in 1974, Fear has returned many times to knock on the door of my soul. I have learned that if I don't open the door, he can't get in.

Worth repeating: A wise person once said, "Fear knocked at the door. Faith opened it. No one was there." (source unknown)

Today's prayer: *"Dear Lord, You know my struggle with Fear. Thank You that I can depend on Your faithfulness. I ask for Your powerful peace to protect me and rule over my life. I turn my worries and problems over to You right now. Amen."*

Ruth's double love story

retold by María Luisa Navarro

The Bible tells a double love story in the book of Ruth.

During the 300 years when Israel was ruled by judges, a famine drove a man named Elimelech and his family from their home in Bethlehem into the country of Moab. There his two sons married local girls.

Then Elimelech and both his sons died, leaving Elimelech's widow, Naomi, and her two daughters-in-law with no one to support them. Naomi decided to go back to Bethlehem, where she had relatives and where the famine had ended.

Naomi urged her daughters-in-law to stay with their own people. It would be easier for them to remarry in their native country, Moab, and besides, the Israelites looked down on people from Moab as heathen. The first girl agreed, but the second one, Ruth, refused to leave Naomi. "I want to go wherever you go and live wherever you live," she said. "Your people shall be my people, and your God shall be my God."

So Naomi and Ruth made their way back to Bethlehem, where they were soon close to starving.

In the surrounding fields, a fine crop of barley was being harvested. Now, in those days in Israel, the law permitted poor people to follow reapers in the field and pick up stray stalks of grain. Ruth decided to glean this free grain in a field belonging to a rich man named Boaz, a distant relative of Naomi's. While Ruth was gleaning, Boaz arrived. "Who is that woman?" he asked his foreman.

"That's the foreigner from Moab who came with her mother-in-law, Naomi," he said. "She has been working all day and has only stopped a few minutes to rest."

So Boaz went over to Ruth and invited her to continue working in his fields, where she would be safe and secure. She thanked him, and then asked why he was treating her so kindly when she was a foreigner.

"You may be a foreigner," Boaz said, "but I have heard about all the love and kindness you have shown to your mother-in-law, Naomi, since both your husbands died. I know you left your father and mother in your own land to come here to live among strangers to help her. May the Lord God of Israel, under whose wings you have come to take refuge, bless you for this."

Intrigued by this woman, Boaz invited her to lunch the next day and then showered her with food to take back to Naomi. Privately, he told his young men to snap off some heads of barley and drop them on purpose for Ruth to gather. "And don't make any remarks to her," he warned.

That evening, Ruth returned to Naomi with a whole bushel of barley. When she told her mother-in-law all about Boaz's kindness to her, Naomi cried, "Boaz! He is one of our closest relatives!"

As harvest time drew to a close, Naomi told her daughter-in-law that it was time for her to think of marriage— to Boaz, who had continued to be so kind to them. Then she advised Ruth how to proceed according to Israelite customs of that day.

"Dress up and go to the threshing floor," she said. This is where Boaz would be sleeping that night to protect his crops. "Then lie down at his feet." Boaz would understand this action as Ruth's desire for him to marry her, as her deceased husband's next of kin, to raise children to carry on the family name.

When Ruth did as Naomi advised, Boaz said, "You are being even kinder to Naomi now than before. Naturally you would prefer to marry a younger man than me, even if he was poor. But you have put aside your personal desires."

By then Boaz was completely taken by Ruth's inner beauty and determined to marry her. However, custom decreed that a closer relative of Naomi's than Boaz had to be offered the first chance to marry her. So Boaz formally went before the city elders to ask this man if he was willing to marry Ruth. Fortunately, this relative already had a family, so he turned down that honor and responsibility.

Boaz married Ruth, and the Lord gave them a son, Obed. When Obed was born, the women of the city came to Naomi and said, "Bless the Lord who has given you this grandson! May he be famous in Israel. May he restore your youth and take care of you in your old age. For he is the son of your daughter-in-law, who loves you so much and has been kinder to you than seven sons."

In time, Obed became the father of Jesse and the grandfather of Israel's famous King David. Truly, Ruth was blessed many times over for her love and her faithful responsibility to Naomi.

Worth repeating: *"But the fruit of the Spirit is love, joy, peace, patience, kindness, goodness, faithfulness, gentleness and self-control"* (Gal. 5:22–23a).

Today's prayer: *"Lord, please develop in me Ruth-like qualities, that I might find favor with You and with others. Amen."*

A welcome for Kenny

by Kathryn Knight-Chapman

In September 1980, I was blessed with the birth of a son, Kenny. Unfortunately, my child's biological father and paternal grandparents denied that Kenny was theirs. They have never laid eyes on him nor acknowledged him in any way. If it had not been for the love and support of my parents, I honestly do not know what would have happened to Kenny or me.

When Kenny was 8 years old, God blessed me once again. I met Randy Chapman. He loved me, and he loved Kenny as if Kenny was his own, biological child, too. Kenny fell so in love with Randy, that even before we were married, he started calling him "Dad."

When Randy and I decided to get married, I was nervous about taking Kenny to Hobbs, New Mexico, to meet my future in-laws, Larry and Jean Chapman. But they put us at ease. When Randy introduced his mother to my son, Kenny said, "Hello, Mrs. Chapman."

"No, no!" she said, hugging him. "I am your Grandmother Jean."

They just accepted us. We were part of the family. They treated Kenny exactly like their other grandchildren—as if they had known him all their lives.

My dad's favorite story about Larry Chapman, whom we called Paw, happened on a plane. We bought my dad and Paw tickets to fly with Kenny to Phoenix to see a pro football game. The two grandfathers were separated from Kenny by an aisle seat, and my dad kept leaning forward to check on him.

Finally the man seated next to Kenny pierced my dad with a questioning look. "He's my grandson," Dad explained.

"No," Paw immediately corrected him, "he's OUR grandson."

My precious father-in-law was taken from us suddenly. He and Grandmother Jean were visiting Paw's brother's family in Oklahoma, and somehow the gas or water heater in their mobile home fell through the trailer floor. Paw realized carbon monoxide was leaking into the mobile home. He woke up his wife, brother, brother's wife, and nephew. Then he got them outside and called 911.

Paw died of massive carbon monoxide poisoning. He saved the lives of four people and paid with his own. He was only 58.

Paw used to buy Kenny little gifts, and he started Kenny collecting baseball cards. When Paw died, my husband and his siblings packed up their father's belongings. In his suitcase they found a box of baseball cards, tagged "To Kenny from Paw."

At Paw's funeral Mass, Randy and I wanted so much to stand up and tell people about Paw's caring, sensitive, and loving nature, but we were too overcome with grief. Today, we are still grieving, still regretting that we were too weepy to tell people about the love story between Kenny and Paw.

Then I read the paragraph at the end of this column saying that people could share their stories. So I thought, "Maybe this is my chance to tell that story."

My son started out life being denied by some of the ones who should have loved him. I believe that he is the successful young man he is today because of the love and guidance he has been shown by his angelic grandparents, Fred and Naomi Knight, Jean Chapman, and, in loving memory, Larry Chapman. Thank you all, and thank you Paw.

Worth repeating: *"Children's children are a crown to the aged, and parents are the pride of their children"* (Prov. 17:6).

Today's prayer: *"Lord, I want to live a life like Larry Chapman's that makes my children proud that I'm their parent. I am willing to make whatever changes You show me I need to make, in order for that to happen. Amen."*

& **The story behind this story:**

A sentence at the close of each "Year of the Family" column gave a phone number for readers who wanted to share their own stories. When Kathryn noticed it, she sat right down and wrote a tribute to her father-in-law, then phoned to ask if she could share her family story. We worked on it together then to prepare it for publication. Kathryn said later that writing the tribute helped her grieve her father-in-law's death. - ed.

The loyalty of the orphans

by Becky Cerling Powers

I opened a treasure chest of fascinating stories when my mother's cousin, Laura Richards Nieh, died in 1981. A collection of old letters came to me then, telling about Canaan Home, the orphanage that Laura started in North China in 1929.

Some letters raised questions for me, like the one from U.S. Navy Chaplain Harold Flood. He came to Beijing in 1945 with U.S. Marines to set China free from Japan. He and his men brought food to Canaan Home's 115 orphans, all of whom had somehow survived the terrible famine years of the Japanese occupation. These children ranged in age from tiny babies to teenagers, and they included many severely handicapped children. (Canaan Home took in children who were so severely handicapped that other orphanages in Beijing refused to admit them.)

Chaplain Flood said that Laura and her Chinese husband, Mr. Nieh (whom she married during the occupation), were the only adults taking care of all those children. I thought he must be mistaken. How could that be?

In 1990, I found out. Two former Canaan Home orphans sent me long letters from China describing memories of their childhood. From babyhood, they said, Laura taught them, "The older one helps the younger one, and the stronger one helps the weaker one." As toddlers they learned to do what they could for themselves and then to begin helping others. As they grew, they were given more responsibility.

Before Japan attacked Pearl Harbor, Chinese volunteers helped at the orphanage and taught school lessons. At that time, school-age children attended school half the day and did chores the other half. After the U.S. and Japan declared war on each other, it was too dangerous for Chinese volunteers to help in an American-run facility. So for almost four years, school shut down, and the children doubled up their work day.

Older children supervised younger ones for meals and chores, and they worked in teams of three or four to do all the work needed to keep the family going. They carried water from the spring; tended the garden; cleaned buildings; raised chickens and goats; cooked meals; and sewed, mended, and washed the family's clothes. Laura, who was a nurse, trained the older children to nurse sick children and to care for the babies and handicapped children.

This family cooperation and loyalty helped save these children's lives during the Japanese occupation.

(To the Communists, however, Canaan Home's family loyalty was a threat that had to be destroyed. The story continues on page 124.)

Worth repeating: *"Two are better than one, because they have a good return for their work: If one falls down, his friend can help him up. But pity the man who falls and has no one to help him up!"* (Eccl. 4:9–10).

The loyalty of the orphans

Today's prayer: *"Dear God, help our family to cooperate and to help each other today. Amen."*

📖 The story behind this story:

Laura's story is a buried family tale that nearly died with her, for Laura was a quiet, self-effacing woman who seldom talked about herself. At the retirement home where she spent her last years people thought she was just a sweet old lady who had been a spinster all her life. And although most of Laura's close relatives loved her, she embarrassed them. They believed no respectable white woman would marry outside her own race. When she married Mr. Nieh in 1939 it was a family scandal.

When Laura died, the retirement home sent her belongings to her 86-year-old brother, who died himself a few years later. Her nephews had no interest in her old letters and photographs, so they disposed of them. Fortunately, some copies survived because several years before Laura died, my Aunt Jean (no blood relation to Laura) began drawing out her story. For a short time they worked on a book. Laura gave Jean two extensive interviews along with a few photographs and other materials. The project proved too wearying for Laura, however, and she feared that publishing a book might endanger loved ones still in China. So she dropped the book project, to Jean's disappointment. Later, Laura gave some yellowed old letters to another friend, Fern Nelson, who retyped them to share with friends and family. Fern kept them in a file along with a few memoirs Laura wrote on scraps.

Laura died in 1981, at age 88, and Fern sent my mother copies of Laura's letters. Then Jean died unexpectedly a year later. Her daughter sent Mom Jean's file folder of material. Mom gave all the material to me, and I started researching Laura's story. - ed.

The interrogation of Rosebud and Mama

by Becky Cerling Powers

When Rosebud was 11 months old, her mother threw her out the back door in a fit of anger. So a neighbor in the hill country west of Beijing, China, carried her to Laura Richards, an American missionary who started Canaan Home Orphanage and shared the poverty of the peasants, suffering along with them through famine and war. The neighbors knew that Laura Richards took in orphans and unwanted baby girls.

It was 1935. Little Rosebud was nearly starved, and her spine was injured when her mother threw her. It looked like she would become a little hunchback. To straighten her back, Laura tied her to a slanted board with her feet above her head. Two years later, a Chinese Christian named Mr. Nieh (Nieh Shou Guang) helped Laura rescue Rosebud and the other children from bandits. Later, Laura married Mr. Nieh, and he helped the children survive the Japanese occupation.

In 1949, after a civil war, the Communists took over every office, factory, school, church, hospital, and

The interrogation of Rosebud and Mama

local government. They did this by getting people in each organization to start criticizing and accusing each other until they destroyed their own communities from within. By this time, Canaan Home had grown to 115 children.

In 1950, the Communists physically moved into the orphanage and made all the children attend indoctrination classes. They tried to teach them to stop believing in God and to serve the new People's Republic of China. They also tried to get the children to complain about Laura so they could accuse her in a People's Court. People's Courts were used as an excuse for mob violence. Communists encouraged onlookers to beat up the accused, and thousands were being killed in this way.

In order to find an excuse to accuse the children's Mama Nieh, the Communists questioned the children one by one. But none "cooperated." Finally, they called 16-year-old Rosebud, who had grown up tall, with a good sense of humor.

"When I was a baby, my own mother did not want me," the teenager said. "She threw me out the door and hurt my spine so that I was a little hunchback. But a neighbor brought me to this orphanage, and this mama cured my back." She paused and smiled. "So now I am straight and tall! Now I am strong and ready to help in the People's Recovery!"

Red faced and defeated, the Communists dismissed her. They never could get any of the children to criticize Mama Nieh. They had to figure out a different way to get rid of her.

By early 1951, Laura Richards Nieh was one of the few Americans left in mainland China. After the Communist Revolution, the new government's hostility to foreigners drove most of her missionary and diplomatic friends out of the country. Many left because their simple presence put their Chinese friends' lives at risk. In those days, anyone linked to an American was in danger. Every day throughout the city of Beijing where the family lived, the government staged public rallies, demonstrating against the Korean War and China's chief enemy, the United States. These rallies often turned ugly, with thousands being beaten and killed.

By 1951, Papa Nieh was also in grave danger because his relatives had fought against the Communists in the civil war. The Communists made him attend daily indoctrination classes, and they refused to allow him to be with his wife. He could still run errands in the city, but at home, cadres assigned to Canaan Home monitored him as if he were a prisoner.

Through indoctrination classes, interrogations, and threats, Communist cadres continued to try to make the children criticize their parents and give up their faith in God. Their inability to transfer the orphans' loyalty from God and parents to the Communist regime frustrated and infuriated them. Besides that, they could find no one in Beijing willing to attack or accuse Mama Nieh because of the reputation she had gained among the people.

So finally one day they changed tactics. They called Mama Nieh before them and announced, "If you will accept two conditions, we will allow you to remain head of this orphanage. First, the new government is atheistic, and the children must learn the new ways. So you must no longer tell the children about God. You must no longer mention Jesus or use Jesus to educate the children. Second, you must denounce America. You must recognize and admit that America is the ultra-imperialist country."

"I cannot lie and say there is no God," Mama Nieh replied. "I love the Chinese children. I also love my country."

So Laura had to leave China and her children. Her only comfort was knowing that when she left, the Communist government would stop focusing so much attention on her children. She saw that her presence was now keeping a government spotlight on the orphanage. When she left, the pressure on the children would subside.

For six months Laura waited in Hong Kong for Papa Nieh to escape and meet her. But the Communists caught him and put him in prison. In 1954, they shot him. Laura died at age 88 in 1981. She lived long enough to hear news from some of her children in China and to find out that they had remained loyal to God despite decades of persecution.

Worth repeating: *"Whoever acknowledges me before men, I will also acknowledge him before my Father in heaven. But whoever disowns me before men, I will disown him before my Father in heaven"* (Matt. 10:32–33).

Today's prayer: *"Give me courage and hope, Heavenly Father, to remain always loyal to You. Amen."*

The story behind this story:

Through an unusual series of circumstances, I have been able to contact some of the children of Canaan Home Orphanage. They still live in China and are now in their 60s and 70s. Corresponding and exchanging photographs has been a moving experience. I am grateful to Pastor Timothy Lee and Martin Yee from the El Paso Chinese Baptist Church, who have translated our letters back and forth. Although I have been disappointed not to find a publisher for Laura's story, I was delighted to be able to share part of her story with my city through "Year of the Family." - ed.

Brotherly love

by Sylvia R. Candelaria

I am the only daughter and youngest of five children. My brothers were my mentors and my tormentors. They made sure I knew that my place was to do what they told me, and when. My brothers also loved me dearly. They had unusual ways of showing me love, yet they protected me from the world outside the haven of our home.

One of the greatest gifts they gave me was the confidence to talk to men honestly. In high school, my brother Anthony told me what he wanted and expected of a date—honesty, integrity, and the ability to decide what she wanted to do. Open, honest communication—I thought everyone knew that guys want this, that it was common knowledge.

Farther down the road, in a distant place, I found that my friends did not know this "secret" in talking to guys. It was then that I began to appreciate the prophetic words spoken through my brother. This "common knowledge" of talking honestly with people was not so common.

Too often, we are caught up in our own ideal of what a relationship or friendship should be. Often, it seems, we live in our world of illusions and no one can enter this world. We feel others do not understand us, but who can understand? For who can enter this world of illusions and survive?

As my brother told me, "Be honest...respect yourself." Anthony gave me the self-confidence to speak truth and accept nothing less.

God spoke to me through his messenger Anthony—Anthony, who gave me a black eye with a baseball, who laughed at me, who did not want to be seen in public with me—this messenger who was proud of me as he inducted me into the National Honor Society and introduced me as his sister, who took the time to fly across two states for my high school graduation, who purchased my college class ring, who came to my college graduation, who loves me.

I draw strength from my family as I draw strength from the earth, both evidence of God's unsurpassed love. The oneness in being within my family overcomes the distractions of the world that surrounds us. I don't always agree with family, but I do love them.

Worth repeating: *"Therefore each of you must put off falsehood and speak truthfully to his neighbor, for we are all members of one body"* (Eph. 4:25).

Today's prayer: *"Loving God, let me see You in family and friends. Open my heart to the wonders of Your grace. Amen."*

Smelling the flowers

by Laura Jane Cerling

It was a warm, sultry spring day in Illinois in 1948, and the air was heavy with perfume. I was a young mother with two babies and no car, on my return home from my weekly trek to the grocery store. I still had another mile to walk home.

My 1-year-old, Becky, was inside the baby buggy, along with the groceries. Her 2-year-old sister, Penny, was tired of the buggy ride, so she was slowly loitering on the sidewalk behind me. "Come on, come on," I kept encouraging her. But the distance between us was growing.

Once again I turned around to call her, and this time I saw that she was reaching out for a lovely lavender iris bloom in someone's yard. I started to call out "No, no! Don't take the flower!" But fortunately, before the words could even come out, I realized that my little daughter was being very gentle. Her little face was filled with pleasure as she breathed deeply of the fragrance and softly touched the petals.

"Be still," I told my hurrying self. "She only wants to enjoy what God has made."

It wasn't too long before Penny's little legs were tired, and she was back riding in the buggy. Fifty years have passed, but the memory of those few moments has never left me.

I felt as if God had spoken to me: "Learn from your little girl! Take time to smell the flowers!"

Food for thought: The Bible says, *"unless you change and become like little children, you will never enter the kingdom of heaven...."* (Matt. 18:3). How often do I make time to enjoy God's wonders?

Worth repeating: *"Taste and see that the Lord is good; blessed is the man who takes refuge in him"* (Psalm 34:8).

Today's prayer: *"Lord, thank You for all the beauty surrounding me. Help me to enjoy Your presence in all this beauty with which You have blessed me. Amen."*

A father's love

by Guy Jones

In my first coaching and teaching assignment, I found myself in a small northeastern Colorado town. There I attended a small Methodist church. Among the members was a young couple with a little son who was handicapped with seizures that came without warning.

One day in church, I saw the young boy beginning to have a seizure. His father gently picked him up, held him close to his heart, and patted him on the back, whispering, "That's all right, Son. I love you." I saw no sign of frustration or embarrassment, just the love of this father for his son.

I learned an important message that day. I felt God saying to me, "That's all right, Guy. I love you—even with all your imperfections, all your problems, all your sins—and I am not ashamed or embarrassed to claim you as my son."

Food for thought: I think God is saying that to all of us—that He loves us regardless of the circumstances of our lives. He may not like what we are doing, but His love is always there. I tell the young people I work with that God can close the door on all our yesterdays and open the door to a new life—almost like being "reborn." We can be reborn into a life of joy and happiness, of love and compassion, in the precious name of Jesus Christ.

Worth repeating: The Bible says, *"As a father has compassion on his children, so the LORD has compassion on those who fear him; for he knows how we are formed, he remembers that we are dust"* (Psalm 103:13–14).

Today's prayer: *"Thank You, loving God, for Your compassion for me. I need it. Today I admit to You these my failings, my sins, my limitations: (fill in the blank.). Help me to receive Your forgiveness, mercy, and the power to change. Amen."*

The story behind this story:

Every community is rich with family-building, faith-building stories like this one from Pastor Guy Jones. In El Paso, we were able to fill a daily column with these shared insights after people began to recognize the potential of the stories they passed along to each other in ordinary conversations. Mary Ann Herman and her daughter-in-law, Beth, were trading stories one week about the church services they had attended the previous Sunday. When Beth told Mary Ann a couple of anecdotes that a visiting pastor, Guy Jones, had told during his sermon, Mary Ann said, "Those sound like good stories for the 'Year of the Family' column. Do you think he'd be willing to write them up for us?" She put together a little packet of information about our community writing project, and Beth passed it along to Rev. Jones at a later church service. We were thankful when he took the time to send this story our way. - ed.

Back-up parents

by Janet Allen

As missionary children growing up in Japan, my brother and I missed being part of an extended family, but Mom and Dad reminded us of our family roots back in the States. Mom often told us that if anything happened and we needed help, Paul and I would be looked after by her brother and his wife, Uncle Bob and Aunt Laurie.

Looking back, it might seem like an odd thing to remind a child about often. But because of Mom's serious health problems and the need for international flights if her health deteriorated, my parents wanted to assure us that there was a set of "back-up parents" for us.

Our family came to the States in 1964 when I was 8 years old. It was wonderful to meet our cousins, aunts, and uncles and actually celebrate American/Christian holidays in the United States.

Christmas was an especially thrilling time. I remember getting a tea set and a large walking doll from Grandma and Grandpa Cerling. I remember *lutefisk* and piles of cookies and candies set out on fancy, hand-painted plates Grandma and Grandpa had collected on their trip around the world. It was a feeling I'll never forget, to experience my extended family for the first time.

But my best memory is more recent. My parents had passed away some years before. Something had happened—now I was trying to end my years as a battered wife.

I needed help. So I called. Soon, there were Uncle Bob and Aunt Laurie at the airport. Uncle Bob was barely recovered from emergency heart and gall bladder surgery. Skinny as a rail, he was there to protect me from my abusive 240-pound husband.

It was through that season I learned some valuable lessons. My aunt and uncle showed me that spiritual power is bigger and stronger than anything—like David and Goliath, or Gideon and the enemy camp, or Jesus and the Pharisees. They showed me that it takes special courage to stand with a terrorized, battered woman. People who help can get hurt. They showed that good family is a great treasure.

Mom and Dad were right. If they could not be there, Aunt Laurie and Uncle Bob would take care of me. It was as true when I was 36 as when I was 6.

Worth repeating: The Bible tells us that *"pure and lasting religion in the sight of God our Father means that we must care for orphans and widows in their troubles. What's the use of saying you have faith if you don't prove it by your actions? Suppose you see a brother or sister who needs food or clothing and you say, "Well, good-bye and God bless you; stay warm and eat well—but then you don't give that person any food or clothing. What good does that do?"* (James 1:27; 2:14–16 NLT).

Food for thought: Janet felt that her aunt and uncle demonstrated the reality of their religious convictions by helping in her time of desperate need. They willingly put her welfare above their personal convenience and even their safety.

Today's prayer: *"Dear Lord, open my eyes to see the needs of those around me. Show me specific ways to be there for them. Give me a willingness to get involved and to help others as You guide me. Amen."*

The story behind this story:

For Bob and Laura Jane Cerling's Golden Wedding Anniversary celebration, friends and family sent letters describing their favorite memories of the couple to be collected in a memory book. Their niece, Janet Allen, originally wrote "Back-up parents" as her contribution to that memory book. It was then rewritten slightly a few years later to fit the requirements for the "Year of the Family" column. Quite a few stories for any particular community's "Year of the Family" writing project are probably already in existence, like Janet's tribute, tucked away someplace, just waiting to be discovered and rewritten for publication in the local newspaper. - ed.

Being a real friend

by Kassie Yvonne Roden (age 15)

I, like most people, had a best friend I told everything to. We constantly laughed and gossiped. I completely changed around this friend, and sadly, not in a good way.

My friend seemed so cool and "in" that I tried to dress and talk like her. I started to lie and to be rude to my parents and other adults. I also flirted most of the time. My relationship with God, which had started to grow, eventually began dying.

One day I learned that my friend had talked about me and laughed at me behind my back. I found out that she had been lying to me, also.

What should I do? She had been my friend for some time. I let it go at first, but she did those things again. Finally I realized that a real friend doesn't treat you like that.

The Bible says, *"Spur one another on towards love and good deeds"* (Hebrews 10:24). This means that a real friend is one who will help you along in the right path.

I have tried to forgive my old friend, while at the same time I have changed and tried just to be *myself*. Although finding real friends is hard, it's worth it. I hope I can be that kind of friend.

Worth repeating: The Bible says, *"He who walks with the wise grows wise, but a companion of fools suffers harm"* (Prov. 13:20).

Food for thought: Being hurt by someone we called "friend" can be very painful. We can turn that experience to good, though, by allowing that pain to help us be more sensitive and thoughtful in what we do to others.

Today's prayer: *"Lord, I know how upset I have felt when I've been betrayed by people I have called 'friend.' I don't want to be that kind of friend. Help me to be a true friend, like the friend You are to me. Amen."*

 The story behind this story:
My friend, Karen Ward, invited me to guest teach a few sessions of her creative writing class for young teens in a home school teaching cooperative. Kassie was there and wrote this insightful story for a class assignment. - ed.

Forgiving Grandmother

by Danielle McGill Hinesly

My mama spent hours on a kitchen bar stool crushing vanilla wafers and smashing pecans by hand to blend into her famous chocolate balls. The orange flavoring she added filtered its scent through the house, signaling the beginning of Christmas.

Everyone except my grandmother stole a few. To make sure Mama's rows looked untouched, we had to eat just the right amount, or squish the balls into place so that our thievery wouldn't be discovered. We were naive enough to think Mama didn't know.

One day, not realizing that one of us had hurriedly replaced the pan of Christmas balls on top of the refrigerator, Grandmother opened the refrigerator door. Down crashed the chocolate balls—hours of my mama's hard work ruined. Grandmother waited years to tell us how she chased balls under the table and wiped off the brown dog hair, sprinkling on more sugar so no one would know. She knew her daughter-in-law would be mortified to mail the traditional treats across country after they had shared the floor with the family collie. She spared Mama from having to trash the entire thousand balls and start over.

My grandmother also led a children's Bible study in her small home. Kids squeezed in her front room to see flannel-board stories about Jesus and his love for them. After the children left, Grandmother knelt beside an old gas heater and prayed for each child. When her Bible club kids grew up, they came back often to tell her how much she had blessed them, how much they loved her.

Sadly, I didn't share their tender thoughts. Though I loved Grandmother, I knew her faults, the side of her that the Bible club children didn't see. I couldn't forgive the words with which she occasionally dissected my mother, or the condescending gossip that slipped from her mouth. When she spoke of God's love, I flinched, knowing that her words of God's mercy didn't heal the damage she had inflicted the day before.

Yet, for all that I did know, my ignorance about my grandmother's struggles was greater. In a time when women's health issues were often ignored and mistreated, she suffered from severe migraine headaches which were explained as "all in her head." She and my grandfather also lived on a poverty income that kept her in faded dresses and hand-me-down purses. Despite her chronic pain and lack of money, my grandmother's face still lit up when she saw us walking up her front steps. When my mother died 11 years ago, my grandmother was devastated. She never quite got over it and died within seven months.

Today, I have some of my grandmother's furniture, and I have the tiny diamonds from a sweetheart ring my grandfather gave her. But my most treasured gift is the one she gave to many other children besides me. After my grandmother's death, I discovered that she had spent hours on her knees praying for me. In the midst of human failings, my grandmother did the one thing she could that has brought me love, laughter, and healing. She took time and love to go before God. In the midst of her humanness, she asked God to bless me.

Worth repeating: *"But we have this treasure in jars of clay to show that this all-surpassing power is from God and not from us"* (2 Cor. 4:7).

Today's prayer: *"Lord, I am like an ordinary clay pot — imperfect and easily broken. Fill me with Your Spirit and Your power, I pray. Amen."*

God's therapy for families

by Laura Jane Cerling

"My leg hurts, Mommy," whimpered 2-year-old Lewis Brown. His crying sounded like the fussing of a tired boy to busy Thelma Brown, shopping for groceries in Hazard, Kentucky, with a new baby and her toddler Lewis. Later, though, as she put the children to bed, she noticed that Lewis was still complaining, and now he was limping, too.

This was during the polio scare of the 1950s, and thoughts of polio plagued Thelma's mind as she fell asleep. The next morning she made the long drive into Hazard to take Lewis to the doctor.

"Mrs. Brown, unless I make a painful spinal tap, I can't tell for sure if the boy has polio," the doctor told her. "Your family has already been exposed, so keep him away from others and make him walk. If he's got the disease, that muscle must be kept exercised, or he'll lose it."

Thelma guessed from the doctor's words that he believed her son had the disease, but he felt Lewis could

God's therapy for families

get better care at home than in the hospital in Lexington, 500 miles away where he would have to go if he was officially diagnosed with polio.

It was a time of fear. Hospitals were crowded with polio patients, and people were afraid of catching the disease from them. Polio wards were so understaffed that polio patients had to care for each other. Those who were better cared for those who were the most helpless.

For weeks Thelma forced Lewis to keep walking, crying inside herself as she did it. She hoped her seeming indifference to his pain would not leave a lifelong bad impression on her little boy.

Eventually, Lewis was able to walk normally, but when he reached high school, the family realized that the polio had affected his arms. He was tall and fast and appeared at first to be a good candidate for playing basketball. His arms hurt too much, though, when he lifted them over his head, and he never was able to gain normal strength in his arms.

Years later, Thelma asked Lewis what he remembered about his illness. His only memory was about "the nice black man with the same name as mine who carried me up the doctor's stairs in my stroller."

Food for thought: In later years, as Thelma reflected on this hard time, she realized that God requires her to do hard things sometimes to exercise her spiritual muscles and develop her character, just as she made Lewis keep walking to exercise his physical muscles and avoid becoming crippled.

Worth repeating: The Bible says, *"Endure hardship as discipline; God is treating you as sons. For what son is not disciplined by his father? Our fathers disciplined us for a little while as they thought best; but God disciplines us for our good, that we may share in his holiness. No discipline seems pleasant at the time, but painful. Later* on, however, it produces a harvest of righteousness and peace for those who have been trained by it"* (Hebrews 12:7,10,11).

Today's prayer: *"Heavenly Father, thank You for loving me enough to discipline and train me through life's difficulties. Help me to understand that You are using the problems in my life to exercise my faith in You and to make me a stronger and better person. Amen."*

Teagan's operation

by Mary Ann Herman

It was hard to watch our 4-year-old granddaughter, Teagan, so tiny and helpless in her hospital bed. Her lips quivered every few minutes, even though her mommy had gently explained what would happen. Several nurses had tended to her pre-operation needs and given her cartoon videos to watch.

Teagan refused to look at or even touch the silly paper hat she was supposed to put on for the operation. No coaxing on our part worked.

Judy Ortiz, the OR nurse, strolled to the bed and directed all her attention to Teagan. "My, but aren't you beautiful! You look just like a model," she said. "It's time to go now. Would you like to ride in your bed, or would you rather walk?"

"I'll walk," Teagan whispered.

"Well then, Teagan, that gown you're wearing should be covered. It's sort of open in the back. Let's wrap you up in this blanket. Just stand up on the bed. I'll get you all fixed up real glamorous," Judy said.

Then Judy picked up the hat. "Oh, Teagan, you've got such beautiful hair! I think you'd better wear this nice hat. So many of our doctors are either bald or have only a little hair. They might be jealous if they saw your lovely hair."

Teagan agreed to all Judy's suggestions. She even put on the silly hat. Judy helped Teagan off the bed, and then said, "Let's sashay down this hall, Teagan. We'll show everyone how gorgeous we are."

Teagan was so engrossed in Judy's theatrics that she didn't even bother to wave to Mommy or Poppa or me. Later we heard that when they arrived in the operating room hand in hand, Judy announced, "Ta da! Here we are!"

The surgery went well, and Teagan is recovering nicely. I was so grateful to the surgical staff at Columbia West, but particularly was thankful for Judy, who performed a miracle in changing a scary episode into a happy adventure.

Judy and her colleagues showed that we should always show respect to others, including our precious little ones. Just watching Judy with Teagan made me teary-eyed. Here's a nurse who focused herself totally on Teagan's needs at an anxious time. Those "Judy Ortiz" dramatics were filled with love, caring, and kindness.

Food for thought: How we treat others, especially the weak and helpless among us, is the yardstick for measuring our character.

Worth repeating: The Bible says that one day the disciples were arguing about which of them would be the greatest in the kingdom of God. *"But Jesus knew their thoughts, so he brought a little child to his side. Then he said to them, 'Anyone who welcomes a little child like this on my behalf welcomes me, and anyone who welcomes* me welcomes my Father who sent me. Whoever is the least among you is the greatest'" (Luke 9:47,48 NLT).

Today's prayer: *"Dear Lord, help me to be kinder and more caring. Make me sensitive to the fears of others and show me how to put them at ease. Make me a blessing to all the people, young and old, that I meet today. Amen."*

📖 The story behind this story:

Mary Ann's story about her granddaughter's operation was published several weeks after the surgery. One day, Teagan and her mother, Beth, were waiting in line at a drive-up bank. To pass the time, Beth was paging through the *El Paso Times* and listening to a local radio station when she heard the DJ say, "If my son is ever in the hospital, I want Nurse Judy Ortiz to take care of him!" Then the DJ told listeners to read the story about Judy Ortiz and Teagan in the "Living" section of the *El Paso Times*. Beth flipped to the story. "You're in the newspaper, Teagan!" she said, and read her the column. Teagan was excited. What a special gift from her grandmother! - ed.

Refugees wandering

by Laura Jane Cerling

Our friend, Horst Hehr, grew up in the chaos of wartime Europe, which turned out to be good preparation for his work today as a hospital chaplain.

Like many European families, Hehr's family was uprooted over and over during World War II. Young Hehr traveled trustfully from place to place, going wherever his mother went. But she must have often wondered whether or not the family would ever find a safe place to live and prosper.

Several generations before, Hehr's German ancestors had settled in Bessarabia (now part of Romania) at the invitation of Catherine the Great, a German princess and widow of the Russian Czar, Peter II. Hehr's ancestors were Protestants who moved to avoid persecution for their faith in Germany.

In 1939 many shifts of power occurred in Europe. The dominant players were Italy, Germany, and Russia. Stalin and Hitler agreed that Russia would be allowed to control Bessarabia while Germany attacked Poland. In

Refugees wandering

1940, Russia gave German residents in Bessarabia an ultimatum: either stay in the land and submit to Communist rule or leave within 30 days. Staying would have meant losing their property and religious freedom. Opposition would have meant immediate death.

Horst Hehr was the fifth and last generation of his family to live in Bessarabia. He was 2 years old when his family moved to conquered Poland.

In 1942, Hehr's father died, and his coffin was placed in the main room for family and friends to view the body. When no one else was there, 4-year-old Hehr and his 3-year-old sister crept into the room. They stood on a chair, gazing into the coffin, and they both cried and cried. No one silenced or questioned them.

That childhood experience helped Hehr accept death and dying. It also helped him comfort many people years later when he became a chaplain for sick or grieving patients and patients' family members. He'd learned as a young child that deep feelings of sorrow need to be felt and shared.

Young Hehr learned other lessons as well, as the war intensified.

In the fall of 1944, 6-year-old Hehr began to notice groups of women marching by in formation every day, carrying shovels. When he asked his mother about them, she said, "These are Jewish women who are being forced to dig trenches to keep the Russian tanks from coming closer."

One day, during apple harvest, a farmer began tossing windfall apples to the passing women. They scooped them up and started eating them. Then, to Hehr's horror, the soldiers guarding the women began to curse and beat them.

Why wouldn't the soldiers let those women eat the apples? For years Hehr pondered that scene, trying to make sense of it, as children do. He never forgot it. Although he was a child, he knew it was evil.

It was now two years since Hehr's father had died, leaving his mother a widow with four children caught between warring armies. Allied forces were bombing Germany around the clock and advancing on Hitler's tottering regime. The Russians were closing in on Poland. Once again Hehr's family faced the threat of Communist rule.

His mother, aunt, and grandparents decided to flee to territory controlled by either the Americans or British. Polish neighbors helped his mother prepare a wagon, and the family began their dangerous journey soon after Christmas 1944.

The family tried to travel in wooded areas and along side roads to avoid being noticed. But in order to cross over a river, they had to pass through a city with a bridge. As the family neared the city at dusk, air raid sirens began screeching a warning of approaching bombers. Hehr's mother stayed with the horse and wagon, while his aunt took the four children into a wooded area for protection.

Bombs whistled, then exploded. Some bombs fell by the wagon, but fortunately these were duds. At dawn, the family traveled through the city, passing through a major railway center and over the city's bridge, both targets of the bombing raid. Had the raid succeeded, they would have been unable to escape.

On they went, traveling for two months to the war zone of West Germany. Three weeks after arriving, they had to barricade themselves in their government-assigned, basement apartment during a major battle. Then for several years after Germany's surrender, the family of five lived in a bedroom and a kitchen.

During this time of scarcity, Hehr's mother and grandparents became concerned about the children's future because refugee children were not permitted opportunities for advanced education. A German who had lived in the United States told Hehr's mother she should take her family to America.

Although Hehr's grandparents knew they might never see their grandchildren again if she did, they encouraged her to go. The grandfather had lost his farm and country in 1940, and now he could get work only as a poorly paid manual laborer. "Go where the children can get a professional education," he told his daughter. "Then when the land is taken from them, they will be able to start over."

The grandmother had a deep faith in Jesus and urged her daughter to trust him for her needs in America. So, Hehr's mother applied to go.

Meanwhile in Minnesota, a Christian farmer inherited a farm. "How can I express my thanks to God for giving me this farm?" he asked his pastor.

The pastor suggested he sponsor a refugee family and showed him a list of people needing sponsors. The farmer looked it over until he found just the right family — a widow with four children. "No one else will want this family," he explained, "because they have no man to do the heavy work."

So the farmer and his wife took in Hehr's family. Hehr attended high school in Minnesota, and then went on to college and seminary. Today he is Protestant chaplain for the Mercy Medical Center system hospitals in Clinton, Iowa. His life experiences have given him understanding and compassion for the sick and grieving people he counsels.

Food for thought: Great trials prepare for great service.

Worth repeating: The Bible says, *"Weeping may remain for a night, but rejoicing comes in the morning"* (Psalm 30:5b).

Today's prayer: *"Thank You, God, that You can use even our sorrows to do Your work. Amen."*

Dan's tree

by Mary Ann Herman

One chilly, damp spring day our 11-year-old son, Dan, taught me a lesson in faith. Dan came home from school all excited. "Mom, guess what? We all got trees to plant. See, here's mine. Can I plant it now?"

Dan's treasure was a scrawny twig. I didn't have the heart to say what I was thinking, *No way will that grow.* Instead I said, "What a fine project. Why don't you put it in the refrigerator? Change into your play clothes and then you can plant your tree."

"How tall do you think it will get, Mom? Where should I plant it?" Dan asked, as he gently laid the twig on a shelf in the refrigerator.

I was busy and didn't answer except to say, "Remember that wherever you plant it, protect it with a little fence so the dog won't disturb it or go to the bathroom on it."

Soon Dan rushed into the kitchen in his play clothes, took his twig, and announced, "I'll get Dad's shovel."

Dan's tree

I watched him from the kitchen window and smiled at his confidence. He patiently dug a hole in the back yard, planted the tree, and then fenced it in with a circle of left over chicken wire. "Mom, come and see up close," yelled Dan. I dashed outdoors to praise him for his work. He'd done a fine job and even cleaned the shovel before storing it.

A few weeks later, Dan's scrawny twig was sprouting. Dan checked on it every day, and watered it carefully. He liked to show his friends how "my tree is growing." That tree was an important part of Dan's life.

Two years later, my husband was transferred out of state to a new job. We sold our home with Dan's five-foot tree in the back yard. Former neighbors kept us posted on the tree's growth. The last we heard, Dan's tree was taller than the roof of the house.

It's been 25 years since that little boy showed his mother a true act of faith. My in-family joke is, "Whenever I really want something to happen, I just do a Dan!"

Food for thought: I'm glad I didn't voice my doubt when Dan proudly showed me his scrawny little tree. I'm even gladder Dan had faith to follow through, plant his tree, and believe it would grow. What can you do today to encourage the hopes of your children? What step of faith will you take this day toward fulfilling your own dream?

Worth repeating: What is faith? The Bible defines it this way: *"It is the confident assurance that what we hope for is going to happen. It is the evidence of things we cannot yet see"* (Hebrews 11:1 NLT).

Today's prayer: *"Dear Father, thank You for the dream You have put in my heart. Help my faith in You to grow stronger so that together we might achieve this dream. And please show me ways to keep encouraging the hopes of others. Amen."*

Foster grandparent

by Jennifer Cummings

"You've got to quit that Foster Grandparent Program," Yolanda Luna's husband tells her. "You come home crying too often." But Grandmother Luna thanks God for leading her into the program.

"I love children, and these children especially need me," Grandmother Luna says. She has been in the Foster Grandparent Program six years and is currently on assignment at the El Paso Shelter for Battered Women.

Grandmother Luna recalls the story of a 6-year-old foster grandson. "At the beginning of the school year everything was fine. He worked, played, and was happy. But then he became aggressive and had tantrums. One day, he clenched his fists and buried his face in my chest, saying, 'I want to kill myself!'"

The boy's parents, in the midst of divorcing, were too involved with their own struggles to notice that their child was seriously disturbed. That was one of the days that Grandmother Luna went home crying.

Shelter children are victims of family violence. They witness abuse between their parents and are abused sometimes themselves. Grandmother Luna listens, reads stories, helps with homework, plays games, and gives lots of hugs. The children show their love for her by bringing gifts of artwork, candies, and small wrapped surprises. Sometimes this makes Grandmother Luna cry, too.

Some children become attached to Grandmother Luna, clinging and refusing to go to the lunchroom, classes, or playground. Grandmother Luna promises to be with them whenever she can, but tells them, "Don't worry, you are so precious you have your own special angel with you all of the time."

Each small step toward healthy independence is a giant achievement that can bring tears of joy to Grandmother Luna.

Grandmother Luna is proud of her own 17-year-old granddaughter, Christine. "She is a good student and earned a scholarship to Loretto," she says. "Christine does her homework before she goes to the mall or talks on the telephone. In her freshman year, she earned attendance at a six-week math camp in Colorado. Her school sponsored this summer's trip to Kentucky. In October, she will go to Washington,DC, to spend time with one of the Texas senators. I am so happy that she is doing well."

Grandmother Luna has experienced first hand the effects on children of good and bad family life. Stable, loving, peaceful families like her own grow emotionally healthy children like Christine. Violent, drug-dependent, chaotic families grow emotionally disturbed children. Yes, Grandmother Luna does shed tears for neglected children because she knows there is a better way. Each day at the shelter she gives the children a glimpse of hope for a happier future.

Worth repeating: "But the Lord's love for those who respect him continues forever and ever, and his goodness continues to their grandchildren ...." (Psalm 103:17 NCV).

Today's prayer: "Dear God, many homes are broken, violent, and lacking in love and respect. Grandmother Luna gives hope to hopeless children. Help us join her in working toward strong, healthy families. Amen."

Give me a perfect child, Lord

by Janet M. Crowe

There he goes again, I thought to myself. *Why do they let that child sing so loudly?*

It was a difficult time in my life, filled with disappointment over my husband's and my unsuccessful efforts to conceive a child. Every Sunday I apologized to God for my impatience with His timing and, in the same breath, pleaded with Him for a child. Whenever I started to feel a bit of inner peace, a baby would cry. Each tiny cry pierced my heart.

I heard him again. Half a beat late came the voice of someone singing just a little too loudly and slightly off key. As I had done on Sundays past, I searched for the source of the noise. The boy sat with his family in the front pew. I didn't understand why his family allowed him to sing in such a distracting manner. Surely they noticed how loud he was.

It was then that the woman in front of me left with her small child, clearing a space and making it possible for the first time for me to catch more than a glimpse of the noisy boy. He was 10- or 12-years old, and he had Down syndrome.

Shame slapped me in the face, as I remembered the way I had scorned his singing. I recalled all my many prayers asking God to bless me with a child, a healthy child with no problems or handicaps. Weakly, I sat down.

Almost audibly, Christ's words in Matthew 21:16 (NAB) scolded me, *"Did you never read this, 'From the speech of infants and children you have framed a hymn of praise?'"*

Sitting on the edge of my pew, I watched this child. His attention never left the altar. Intently, his eyes followed the priest's every movement, straying occasionally to look at the crucifix hanging behind the priest. I caught my breath to see the pure love and worship reflected in his eyes. "Let us give thanks to the Lord our God," said the priest.

"It is right to give him thanks and praise," the boy enthusiastically responded.

His words came just a second later than the rest of the congregation, as if he were slightly out of step. Then I realized that it was not he, but the rest of us, who were out of step. This child was speaking the words with the tenderness of adoration, rather than our familiar routine responses.

I watched the boy's eyes and face as he truly participated in the celebration of the Mass, and as I watched his expression, an understanding of the depth and fullness of God's love for each of us overwhelmed me. When we began the Lord's Prayer, I felt that Jesus was teaching me to pray by allowing me to see God's love reflected in the boy's eyes.

Christ's repetition of the psalmist's words in Psalm 8:3 (NAB) sounded again in my ears, *"Out of the mouths of babes and nurslings you have fashioned praise."*

Words from a familiar hymn about God's forgiveness lifted my spirit. As always, the childish voice of the boy in the front pew sang slightly slower and louder than everyone else. This time, however, I could almost see the angels in heaven singing, not with the choir's trained voices, but joining with the young boy's pure and heart-felt song of praise.

Food for thought: This child could not hit the high notes, but he understood that God listens with His heart.

Today's prayer: *"Dear Lord, help me to see with Your eyes, to listen with Your ears, and to love with Your heart. Help me to love You with the simple purity of a child. Amen."*

Deciding to adopt

by Vicky Clingermayer

My feelings of joy and love for Jim overflowed, coloring everything I saw and turning the garden that we were walking through into the most beautiful place on earth. We sat on a bench surrounded by white flowers, drinking in the fragrance and beauty around us and basking in the friendship and love that refreshed us.

We were planning to be married in several months, and our conversation drifted to the family we knew God would give us. We both wanted children.

"Vicky, what do you think about adoption?" Jim asked. "I think it's essential that we do something more than just talk about the importance of choosing life for the unborn."

I agreed. As a child I had made gifts to take to an orphanage, and I'd always had it in my heart to do something for children without family and love.

Then, three days before our wedding, my doctor told me, "You have an intrauterine fibroid tumor.

Surgery is not recommended. It is more effective when the tumor is larger. But even then, there is no guarantee that you will ever be able to have children. Try not to become pregnant yet. There's too much risk involved."

I wept when I told Jim. "It's OK, Vicky," he said, his warm love cradling my broken heart. "I love you. Remember how we talked about adoption?"

"Thank You, God," I breathed. "Thank You for Jim."

I was sure, though, that God would provide us with children after we married, and I prayed constantly for them, for their future spouses, and for the grandchildren we would have someday. My prayers were a mixture of desperation and longing and of hope in Someone and something larger than I. They were emotionally similar to the prayers I had lifted up at 32 years of age, still single, wanting to be married. "Lord," I had cried then, "You know the best man in the world for me. Lead us together. Prepare our home for the children You want us to have."

• • •

"I had a tumor the size of a grapefruit removed," a new friend told me one day. Her swollen belly was heavy with new life. I quickly took down the phone number of her doctor.

At my appointment, his words encouraged me. "Try to become pregnant," he said. He'd read in a recent medical journal that, for someone with my condition, the chances of carrying a baby to term were good. Also, a possibility existed that the pregnancy itself could decrease the size of the tumor.

But after numerous check-ups, procedures, and visits to specialists, I did not become pregnant. My belly became larger, but only because the tumor was growing. Finally, my doctor said there was danger of hemorrhage. A date was set, and the surgery was performed.

With family and friends beside him in the waiting room, the doctor told my husband Jim, "Vicky's tumor was the size of a soccer ball, and her ovaries were stretched out of shape and covered with endometriosis. We had to remove everything."

Jim wept, not so much for the children we could no longer have, but for me. I had hoped and trusted. Now those hopes were gone. Would that trust remain?

Friends and family sent flowers and cards, wishing me well and encouraging me to "hang in there." They assured me of their prayers. I felt strangely peaceful. Surely God would replace the emptiness of my womb in His way, with His provision.

While I was grieving, God did provide an outlet. A 2-year-old adopted by a friend a few weeks after my surgery kept me busy. While she went to work, I watched her precious child. My days were full. I thanked God in advance for his provision for children for Jim and me.

The months following my hysterectomy were difficult, especially at family gatherings. "God," I cried, "I asked for children. Even before I was married, I prayed for the children You would give us someday."

At Christmas it seemed there were children everywhere. My sister had visited from out of state, and one evening I shared with her all my grief, confusion, and hurt. The next evening she told me, "Vicky, I would be willing to carry your baby for you. Steve says it's OK."

As a nurse, I knew she understood the ramifications of her offer. This was my answer! I knew it was! God had answered my prayers in a most unlikely way! I couldn't wait to share my joy and excitement with Jim.

But he said, "No."

I couldn't believe what I was hearing. Surely he didn't mean it. I sobbed and argued.

"We can't always have what we want when we want it!" His words stung. "We have to consider others, too,

Deciding to adopt

not just ourselves. Maybe our inability to have children is God's way of providing for a child who needs a loving family."

I couldn't help but see the truth in his words. Hadn't God prepared us for this? After all, we had talked about adoption even before I knew I couldn't bear children. Once again I prayed, "Heavenly Father, You know all things. You know my children even though they may not yet have been conceived. Give us who You want, Lord, and teach us Your way.'

But the grief remained. Emptiness rocked me to sleep at night, even as I prayed for children.

We began applying for adoption. We talked with an agency that gave us forms to discuss and fill out together. Two weeks later, almost finished, we read the final question at the kitchen table: "Describe the kind of child you would be willing to adopt."

Both of us agreed that because every life is a gift from God, our response would be open. "We are willing to take any child who needs a home, as God leads us," we wrote.

Just as we completed this last question, the phone rang. "Are you still interested in adopting a baby?" our caller asked. We hadn't heard from this friend for over a year. We listened, unbelieving, as she told us that a young mother needed a home for her baby, due in September.

"Yes," we stammered, asking questions excitedly. There was a fullness to that moment that bubbled over and covered all our questions, fears, and emptiness.

Soon we were talking to the birth mother by phone. Having been adopted herself as a child, she felt this was the best decision for her baby. She sounded sure and peaceful about her decision.

That night Jim and I couldn't sleep. We held each other and prayed, "Thank You Lord! How abundantly You have provided for us. Now walk with us into the future. Amen."

Update: Today, as the parents of three adopted children, we continue to pray this prayer, and we recommend it to you.

Worth repeating: The Bible says, *"Now faith is being sure of what we hope for and certain of what we do not see"* (Hebrews 1:1). *"And we know that in all things God works for the good of those who love him, who have been called according to his purpose"* (Romans 8:28).

Lofty pine

by Paula Kortkamp Harvie

The majestic old yellow pine in the mountains of New Mexico stood tall and stately. We always felt privileged it was on our property. Its base measured 13 feet around; its lofty branches towered above all other trees in the area.

If trees could talk, this one could tell quite a story, for it was already a young sapling during Spain's rule over New Mexico. When the United States of America was born in 1776, the tree was more than 50 years old. By the time New Mexico became the 47th state in our Union, this noble sentry had already stood guard in the forest over 200 years. It had weathered the changing seasons; it had survived countless storms and adversities. For nearly three centuries it had silently but faithfully pointed man's attention upward to its Creator.

I found inspiration in the great pine. Looking at its staggering height, I often prayed, "Lord, help me to grow spiritually like that tree, tall in faith, strong in adversity, faithful in pointing others to You."

My Roots Go Back to Loving

Then one spring day a few years ago, we found sap oozing from the trunk of the stately giant. I made a mental note to have it checked, but somehow other things crowded out my good intentions.

During the following months sap continued to pour from numberless holes in the bark. Yes, I must have the tree sprayed, I thought every time we visited the cabin. One day our son came home from the cabin very concerned. "Mom, do something about that tree!"

"Yes, Jon, I will." But I didn't. I meant to, but I was busy. Summer became fall, and then it was winter. I forgot about the tree.

Returning to our cabin the following spring, I was shocked and ashamed to see the sad condition of the grand old giant of the forest. Its needles had turned brown; sap flowed down its mighty trunk, pooling on the ground. Alarmed, I called tree experts, but it was too late. An infestation of the pine beetle had struck the Lincoln National Forest and killed our magnificent tree. Today its huge stump serves as a grim reminder of the high cost of ignoring small problems.

Food for thought: For nearly 300 years the big tree had successfully survived all major tests, only to fall victim to a tiny insect that had secretly bored into its core. The lesson of the tree is this: Nations, like trees, may be great and mighty, but if they ignore the tiny insects of immorality infesting their core, they risk certain destruction. Likewise, individuals who tolerate small, secret sins infecting their character invite a similar fate.

Worth repeating: The Bible, comparing sin to yeast, says, *"It is not right for you to be proud! You know the saying, 'A little bit of yeast makes the whole batch of dough rise.' You must take out this old yeast of sin so that you will be entirely pure"* (1 Cor. 5:6-7 TEV).

Today's prayer: *"Dear Lord, forgive me for ignoring the secret sins in my life and for tolerating the moral problems infecting my nation. Help me to deal with them while there is still time. Please have mercy on me and on our great country. Amen."*

Index of Writers and Storytellers

Acton, Debbie
    Practical jokes   44
Allen, Janet
    Back-up parents   134
Bulthuis, Peter
    Susan's monkey   66
    The family secret   28
Candelaria, Sylvia R.
    Brotherly love   128
Cerling, Laura Jane
    Glad I listened   105
    God's therapy for families   142
    Refugees wandering   148
    Rescuing Joash   58
    Smelling the flowers   130
    Start the day with love   23
Clingermayer, Vicky
    Deciding to adopt   160
Crowe, Janet M.
    Give me a perfect child, Lord   157
Cummings, Jennifer
    Aunt Virginia   63
    Calling Pepsi   34
    Foster grandparent   154
    Giving comfort   14
    Grandma thinks fast   80
    Susie's first funeral   100
    Turning 50   53
Diaz, Francis A.
    Early lessons pay off   85
Fierro, Ruben
    Mama's prayers   12
Hart, Noel
    The family I needed   51
Harvie, Paula Kortkamp
    Dreaming of Anita Jo   82
    Faith vs. fear   111

Index of writers and storytellers

Harvie, Paula Kortkamp, *continued:*
    Lofty pine   165
    Lost and found cousins   21
    Miracle baby   48
    Psalm 91: antidote to insomnia   91
    The mysterious patient   69

Herman, Joe
    Focusing on the good stuff   5

Herman, Mary Ann
    Dan's tree   152
    Growing up in an orphanage   25
    Teagan's operation   145

Herrington, Annette Horton
    Praying for rain   55

Hinesly, Danielle McGill
    Forgiving grandmother   139

Jones, Guy
    A father's love   132

Jones, Rosie Chavarria
    Recovery from abortion   75

Knight-Chapman, Kathryn
    A welcome for Kenny   118

Markel, Katherine Blake
    Chocolate pie mistake   10

Martinez, Daniel
    My roots go back to Loving   16

McKenzie, Zula
    Grandma's Christmas in July   108

Mims, Herb
    Praying for a little brother   19

Navarro, María Luisa
  as told to stories:
    Mama's prayers *(Ruben Fierro)*   12
  retold stories:
    Ruth's double love story   114

Nodjimbadem, Néaouguen
    Rescuing my family from a battlefield   37
    Teaching school during war time   41
    The church is family   88

Powers, Becky Cerling
  as told to stories:
    My two dads *(Janimarie Rowe)*   93
    One border, two families   31
      (Graciela Westeen)
    Practical jokes *(Debbie Acton)*   44
    Recovery from abortion   75
      (Rosie Chavarría Jones)
    Rescuing my family from a battlefield   37
      (Nodjimbadem, Néaouguen)
    Teaching school during war time   41
      (Nodjimbadem, Néaouguen)
    The church is family   88
      (Nodjimbadem, Néaouguen)
  other stories:
    Home schooling chaos   102
    The loyalty of the orphans   121
    The interrogation of Rosebud and Mama   124
    The story behind these stories   1

Powers, Matthew
  Learning at home   60

Roden, Kassie Yvonne
  Being a real friend   137

Roisen, Dianne
  Neighborly love   46

Rowe, Janimarie
  My two dads   93

Schlondrop, Bill
  Catching alcoholism   72

Steely, Virginia Payne
  Mom's mouthwash   98

Ward, Karen M. Pickett
  Saving Butterscotch   8

Westeen, Graciela
  One border, two families   31

Index of Values

Bravery
Refugees wandering, 148; Rescuing my family from a battlefield, 37; Teaching school during war time, 41; Mama's prayers, 12; Saving Butterscotch, 8; Susan's monkey, 66; The loyalty of the orphans, 121; The interrogation of Rosebud and Mama, 124

Caring, compassion
A welcome for Kenny, 118; Back-up parents, 134; Brotherly love, 128; Chocolate pie mistake, 10; Giving comfort, 14; Glad I listened, 105; Growing up in an orphanage, 25; Foster grandparent, 154; Neighborly love, 46; Rescuing Joash, 58; Refugees wandering, 148; Teagan's operation, 145; The loyalty of the orphans, 121; The interrogation of Rosebud and Mama, 124

Cheerfulness
Grandma's Christmas in July, 108; Mama's prayers, 12; Smelling the flowers, 130; Teagan's operation, 145

Commitment
A welcome for Kenny, 118; Aunt Virginia, 63; Back-up parents, 134; Brotherly love, 128; Deciding to adopt, 160; Foster grandparent, 154; One border, two families, 31; My roots go back to Loving, 16; Rescuing Joash, 58; Ruth's double love story, 114; Teaching school during war time, 41; The family I needed, 51; The loyalty of the orphans, 121; The interrogation of Rosebud and Mama, 124

Dependability, trustworthiness
Calling Pepsi, 34; Mama's prayers, 12; Ruth's double love story, 114; Teaching school during war time, 41

Dignity
Mama's prayers, 12; One border, two families, 31; The interrogation of Rosebud and Mama, 124

Encouragement
A welcome for Kenny, 118; Aunt Virginia, 63; Brotherly love, 128; Focusing on the good stuff, 5; Foster grandparent, 154; Learning at home, 60

Faith
Dan's tree, 152; Deciding to adopt, 160; Dreaming of Anita Jo, 82; Early lessons pay off, 85; Faith vs. fear, 111; Give me a perfect child, Lord, 157; Glad I listened, 105; Home schooling chaos, 102; Lost and found cousins, 21; Mama's prayers, 12; Miracle baby, 48; My two dads, 93; Praying for a little brother, 19; Praying for rain, 55; Psalm 91, antidote to insomnia, 91; Recovery from abortion, 75; Refugees wandering, 148; Rescuing my family from a battlefield, 37; Susie's first funeral, 100; The church is family, 88; The interrogation of Rosebud and Mama, 124

Faithfulness
Early lessons pay off, 85; Forgiving Grandmother, 139; Give me a perfect child, Lord, 157; Lofty pine, 165; Mama's prayers, 12; One border, two families, 31; Ruth's double love story, 114; Susan's monkey, 66; Teaching school during war time, 41; The loyalty of the orphans, 121; The interrogation of Rosebud and Mama, 124

Forgiveness
Chocolate pie mistake, 10; Forgiving Grandmother, 139; My two dads, 93; Recovery from abortion, 75; The family secret, 28; The mysterious patient, 69

Friendship
Being a real friend, 137; Chocolate pie mistake, 10; Dreaming of Anita Jo, 82; Giving comfort, 14; Glad I listened, 105; Neighborly love, 46; Practical jokes, 44; Susan's monkey, 66; The loyalty of the orphans, 121

Honesty
Catching alcoholism, 72; Recovery from abortion, 75; The family secret, 28; The interrogation of Rosebud and Mama, 124

Index of values

Honor, respect
A welcome for Kenny, 118; Focusing on the good stuff, 5; Give me a perfect child, Lord, 157; Mama's prayers, 12; My roots go back to Loving, 16; Practical jokes, 44

Humility
Catching alcoholism, 72; Turning 50, 53

Humor
Praying for rain, 55; The interrogation of Rosebud and Mama, 124; Turning 50, 53

Integrity
Catching alcoholism, 72; Lofty pine, 165; Ruth's double love story, 114; The interrogation of Rosebud and Mama, 124

Kindness
Aunt Virginia, 63; Chocolate pie mistake, 10; Focusing on the good stuff, 5; Giving comfort, 14; Neighborly love, 46; Teagan's operation, 145; The family I needed, 51

Love
A father's love, 132; A welcome for Kenny, 118; Back-up parents, 134; Brotherly love, 128; Deciding to adopt, 160; Giving comfort, 14; God's therapy for families, 142; Growing up in an orphanage, 25; Mama's prayers, 12; My roots go back to Loving, 16; My two dads, 93; Neighborly love, 46; Ruth's double love story, 114; Saving Butterscotch, 8; Start the day with love, 23; The family secret, 28; The family I needed, 51; The interrogation of Rosebud and Mama, 124; The loyalty of the orphans, 121; The mysterious patient, 69

Loyalty
Back-up parents, 134; Brotherly love, 128; One border, two families, 31; Ruth's double love story, 114; Susan's monkey, 66; The loyalty of the orphans, 121; The interrogation of Rosebud and Mama, 124

Patience
Chocolate pie mistake, 10; God's therapy for families, 142; Praying for a little brother, 19; Teagan's operation, 145

Perseverance
A father's love, 132; Dan's tree, 152; God's therapy for families, 142; Mama's prayers, 12; Miracle baby, 48; Praying for a little brother, 19; Praying for rain, 55; Teaching school during war time, 41; The loyalty of the orphans, 121

Repentance
Catching alcoholism, 72; Recovery from abortion, 75

Resourcefulness
Grandma thinks fast, 80; Grandma's Christmas in July, 108; Home schooling chaos, 102; Learning at home, 60; Practical jokes, 44; Teagan's operation, 145

Self-discipline
Mom's mouthwash, 98; Start the day with love, 23

Thankfulness
Early lessons pay off, 85; Focusing on the good stuff, 5; Give me a perfect child, Lord, 157; Growing up in an orphanage, 25; Mom's mouthwash, 98; Smelling the flowers, 130; The family I needed, 51

Unity
Lost and found cousins, 21; One border, two families, 31; Refugees wandering, 148; The church is family, 88; The loyalty of the orphans, 121; The interrogation of Rosebud and Mama, 124

Wisdom
Being a real friend, 137; Brotherly love, 128; Giving comfort, 14; Grandma thinks fast, 80; Start the day with love, 23; The interrogation of Rosebud and Mama, 124

About the Editor and Authors

The story writers and storytellers of *My Roots Go Back to Loving* came together with editor and contributing writer, Becky Cerling Powers, in 1998 to tell the city of El Paso their stories through the "1998: Year of the Family" column, then published daily in the *El Paso Times*. The project was conceived when a task force of pastors and civic leaders asked the newspaper to help them promote family values through a daily column written by volunteers. Becky, a former parenting columnist for the *El Paso Times*, coordinated the project with the assistance of Mary Ann Herman.

All 32 story writers and storytellers either live or used to live in the El Paso area, or else they were recruited by El Paso relatives. They range in age from Kassie Roden, who was 15 when she wrote "Being a real friend," to Laura Jane Cerling, who was 77 years old and had six children, eleven grandchildren, and a great-granddaughter. Some of the authors are related. Debbie Acton and Janimarie Rowe are mother and daughter. Mary Ann Herman and Joe Herman are mother and son. Laura Jane Cerling is Becky Cerling Powers' mother, Matthew Powers' grandmother, and Janet Allen's aunt.

Several writers are members of the El Paso Writers' League, the organization that helped to jump start the project. They are Jennifer Cummings, Mary Ann Herman, Zula McKenzie, Dianne Roisen, Bill Schlondrop, and Virginia Payne Steely.

Half of the authors (13 of the 26 story writers) were published for the first time in the "1998: Year of the Family" column.

Give the gift that strengthens families

Check with your local bookstore or order direct

Please send _____ copies of *My Roots Go Back to Loving and other stories from "Year of the Family"* at **$9.95** each (**Texas** residents please use **$10.72** per copy). For shipping and handling costs, add **$3.20** for a single copy or **$4.70** for either 2 or 3 copies. Enquire for shipping and handling on larger orders. I understand that if I am unsatisfied, I may return the book(s) and receive a refund of the purchase price, upon request.

I'm enclosing a check or money order for $_____.
(Make payable to Canaan Home Communications)

Please charge my credit card (circle correct company)

Visa   MasterCard   American Express

number: _____   expiration date: _____

Signature:_____

Name _____

Company (if applicable) _____

Address: _____

City: _____ State: _____ Zip: _____

Telephone: (___)_____ Fax: (___)_____

Email: _____   Orders by mail:

Phone orders: (915) 877-7148
   toll free: (877) 877-2770
FAX orders: (915) 877-5071
Email orders: dwpowers@htg.net

Canaan Home Communications
HC 12, Box 87
Anthony, TX 79821